WINCHESTER SCHOOL OF MISSION

04414

D1463920

'To quote the paraphrase: "God's stre̶̶̶̶̶̶̶̶̶̶̶̶̶̶̶̶̶̶̶̶ ̶̶̶̶̶̶̶̶̶̶̶̶̶̶̶ ̶̶̶̶̶̶est in weak people." This book unpacks that truth in a refreshingly humble, inspiring and personal way. A must-read for aspiring pioneer leaders.'
PHIL POTTER, LEADER OF FRESH EXPRESSIONS

'When the people of the Bible needed to work out their choices and challenges of God and faith they told a story. Paul Bradbury has done the same. Rescuing the ancient wisdom story of 'Jonah and the whale' from children's Bible books where we have too often left it, he has listened, wrestled and travelled with it through his own calling. The result is honest, creative and transforming.'
DAVID RUNCORN, AUTHOR OF DUST AND GLORY (BRF, 2015)

'This is a delightful book from Paul Bradbury. Over several years now of celebrating and working with the gift that pioneers bring, the importance of paying attention to who you are and the gift you bring in relation to God's calling has grown. Bradbury's use of the book of Jonah is a really inspired creative piece of theological reflection. I particularly like the reality of the challenge and struggle in the midst of pursuing calling. We'll be encouraging pioneers at CMS to read this book without a doubt.'
JONNY BAKER, CHURCH MISSION SOCIETY, DIRECTOR FOR MISSION EDUCATION

'Paul Bradbury's Stepping into Grace is a genuinely engaging read. It journeys with the well-known story of Jonah, finding profound and usually unnoticed truths in its familiar lines. It applies them relevantly and winsomely, weaving them together with insights from spiritual giants from the past as well as with the thoughts of contemporary writers from a diverse range of fields. The result is a thought-provoking read where each page is a pleasure. It is a book that encourages, challenges and inspires. It is a book to be read. I'm glad I did—and will do so again in the near future.'
BRIAN HARRIS, PRINCIPAL OF VOSE SEMINARY, PERTH, AND AUTHOR OF COULD THIS BE GOD? (BRF, 2016)

The Bible Reading Fellowship
15 The Chambers, Vineyard
Abingdon OX14 3FE
brf.org.uk

The Bible Reading Fellowship (BRF) is a Registered Charity (233280)

ISBN 978 0 85746 523 8
First published 2016
10 9 8 7 6 5 4 3 2 1 0
All rights reserved

Text © Paul Bradbury 2016
The author asserts the moral right to be identified as the author of this work

Cover image © Phil Jackson; www.harbourviewphotography.com

Acknowledgements
Unless otherwise stated, scripture quotations are taken from The Holy Bible, New International
Version (Anglicised edition) copyright © 1979, 1984, 2011 by Biblica. Used by permission of
Hodder & Stoughton Publishers, a Hachette UK company. All rights reserved. 'NIV' is a registered
trademark of Biblica. UK trademark number 1448790.

Every effort has been made to trace and contact copyright owners for material used in this
resource. We apologise for any inadvertent omissions or errors, and would ask those concerned
to contact us so that full acknowledgement can be made in the future.

A catalogue record for this book is available from the British Library

Printed and bound by CPI Group (UK) Ltd, Croydon CR0 4YY

STEPPING INTO GRACE

moving beyond ambition
to contemplative mission

Paul Bradbury

To Reconnect
and all those who have bravely accepted
the call to journey without maps

Contents

Acknowledgements

Reflections such as these seem clean and polished after the writing of them. However, they are made presentable only through the hard graft of mining in the company of others. I am hugely grateful to have been part of Reconnect, a missional community that has embraced the journey into the unknown that this book explores and has embraced its leader, in all his uncertainty and 'becoming'. Countless conversations over coffee (or something stronger) have been part of the ferment of these pages.

I am also grateful to those who have influenced and commented on my writing as it has developed. Thanks to Fr Martin McGee from Worth Abbey for recommending *Deus Caritas Est* to me so enthusiastically that I couldn't fail to read it. Thanks also to those who generously and honestly made comments on early drafts, in particular Anne Long, Howard Peskett and David Runcorn.

Thanks to Ian Cowley for his enthusiasm and encouragement for the work of Poole Missional Communities and the telling of its story and learning. My thanks to Mike Parsons and colleagues from BRF, with whom working from proposal to manuscript to book has been a delight.

Finally, and most importantly, thanks to Emily, Jacob and Bethany, who have been co-travellers on this trip and without whom I would not be able to journey at all.

Foreword

Pioneer ministry is a sufficiently recent 'rediscovery' in the Church of England that not much has been written reflecting on the experience of actual practitioners. Most of what has been written focuses on the practices or praxis of pioneering. Little has been written about the inner transformation of the practitioner. What does God do within the pioneer to fit him or her for the praxis? What is the spirituality of pioneer ministry?

In *Stepping into Grace* Paul Bradbury corrects this imbalance. Paul is an experienced and able pioneer, reflecting on seven years of ministry in Poole, and interacting with the story of the Old Testament's most unwilling pioneer, the prophet Jonah.

Not everyone is a pioneer, but many Christian leaders embarking on new work in uncharted territory experience similar challenges, walk a similar path and will benefit from Paul's helpful reflections.

There is a spiritual journey that pioneers, and many other disciples, must make, and which they can only make in context. Jesus' disciples learned discipleship when on mission with him, not just in their brief times of retreat with him. They learned through painful mistakes, and (eventually) even through moments of self-deception, just as much as they learned through the times of fruitful ministry and revelation.

Stepping into Grace is a mature reflection on the Holy Spirit's pioneer formation. Transformation for pioneer ministry involves battling the temptations of culture—to do things society's way, the Church's pressure for quick measurable results—and of ministry—finding our identity in experience or status rather than in God. It involves a vulnerability that is the unavoidable condition when starting a new work from nothing. Above all, it requires a mature praxis of discernment, which can only be learned by experience. Discernment is the ability to recognise works of God in which we are to participate. Paul describes his discovery that mature discernment requires a contemplative life and the spiritual disciplines which form it. Who we are, and who we are becoming, is more important than what we know and what we can do. Join him as he shares the journey, which he and his community have made, into such a life.

+Graham Cray

Introduction

One of the most terrifying and yet exciting things in the world is a blank sheet of paper. On some uncertain date in Israel's history a prophet to the king of the Northern Kingdom was given a call to start afresh, start again. Jonah was handed a blank sheet of paper, he was invited to take a journey without maps. His first response was more terror than excitement. His story is a story for anyone called to journey into the unknown with little more than an unshakable sense that they are following the call of God.

Without maps we look for stories, stories that chime with our own developing story, stories that speak into our uncertainty and tell us we are not alone. Jonah has become such a story for me. It is a story that continues to speak from its ancient near-Eastern world into the experiences and challenges of our own. In particular I have found its voice resonating around my experience and vocation in the context of three overlapping worlds.

Firstly, there is the world of the Church. We are in a time when traditional churches face ongoing and threatening decline. There is much anxiety around, as there was in the time of Jonah. Then the once great kingdom of Israel was divided and threatened from every side by vast powers. Before Jonah was called to Nineveh, he sought to speak the voice of God to Jeroboam II, a king whose strategy seemed based on a campaign of restoration, of returning Israel to its former glory, its territory to previous boundaries. In my own tradition, the Church of England, there is considerable anxiety around how we can maintain a system of ministry and pastoral provision that has proved pretty effective for centuries but which is showing significant signs of unsustainability. This system is beginning to put huge pressure on its leaders to provide the same service with less resources. It is urging growth not simply out of a missional imperative but also out of an anxiety about the future. What does this downward pressure from the institution do to the sense of vocation that brought people into ministry in the first place? What if faithfulness to God's call in a particular place and particular time means managing decline, or even death? Will that be honoured, accepted, appreciated? Or what if that same faithfulness means a period of hard, apparently fruitless, labour which prepares the ground for another to sow and perhaps harvest? And what of new ground, on the edge of the current structures? Can those with a passionately held call to be apostles within the Church be given the time, space and resources to experiment, play and sometimes fail, in order to explore what new expressions of discipleship and worship might look like for a new era?

Secondly, there is the world of postmodern, post-Christian Britain. Culturally we have been through a huge shift in the past century, a process of change that accelerated after World War II and continues unabated. In that process of change the Bible, the Church and the moral and spiritual values they guarded and nurtured have been increasingly exiled and relativised. Within this cultural and moral transition, and most significant for what I want to explore, is a shift away from a sense of life as vocation to one of life as utility. We are all infected with a sense that our worth is determined most significantly by our usefulness, what we can achieve, what we can produce. The undermining in our wider culture of a sense of our origins as created in the image of God, and of our purpose as partners in God's ongoing work of creation, has stunted the vocational journey and rendered it nothing more than a race for greater success, greater influence, greater fame or greater reward. It is in this context that the Christian Church has something hugely important, something of immense good news, to say about what it means to be human. The Christian vocational journey of death and resurrection, of dying in order to really live, insists on a deeper inner journey that trumps and ultimately ennobles the competition and ambition, the ladders and races, that characterise much of the modern working world. But to communicate it most profoundly the Church needs, primarily, not only to teach it but to embody it. Jonah is a story of one man's journey towards a true understanding of vocation. It is a story of the providence of God in shaping that transition. It is a story for all time, but perhaps a particularly potent story for our time.

Thirdly, there is my personal world as a pioneer minister. In 2008 my wife Emily and I accepted the invitation to come to Poole in Dorset and take on the challenge of creating new ways of engaging and discipling people with little or no connection with traditional forms of church. We too were given a blank sheet of paper. We too were invited to make a journey into the unknown and to make our own maps. It was my first responsibility within the Church of England and I took it on confidently and with great hope and enthusiasm. It has stretched me, broken me, challenged me, exasperated me and caused me great wonder and excitement in equal measure. It has taken me to places in myself which I could never have anticipated, places into which the book of Jonah, with its story of a vocation stripped, brought to the point of death and then resurrected, began to speak most profoundly. The fact that such a vocational journey has a rich tradition in both the Bible and the history of the Church suggests we are on holy ground and a holy journey. Yet in a church culture of anxiety, where stories of rapid and sensational success can be seized on as motifs for the salvation of the whole Church, this way of descendent, humbling, sacrificial vocation can sound like defeat. Jonah, a book not so much about what Jonah says, or what Jonah does, as what Jonah becomes (and therefore what we might become), is surely an important corrective to this utilitarian virus which has the potential to do huge damage to church leaders. The message of Jonah is that God is more interested in us becoming the people we are created to be than in us doing great things. That does not mean that he cannot do great things through us, nor that doing great things and us becoming who we are are disconnected. The wonder of Jonah is that God does do great things and Jonah is on the road to becoming someone he wasn't at the beginning. And all this takes place through God's mysterious providence and grace, not in a way that can be prescribed or controlled.

For me, at my stage of life and stage of leadership and ministry, this has been a profound message. Furthermore, it isn't a message I have heard elsewhere. There are voices along these lines within the Church and its literature but they are few. I thank God for Eugene Peterson, who has done so much to articulate a holistic and humanising vocational spirituality. He is one giant on whose shoulders I humbly seek to stand. But generally it feels as though church leaders are asked to march to strong tunes, the beat of a strident drum, in the cause of church growth and renewal. Some are weary of this. Some have peeled off and gone elsewhere, perhaps never to return.

There is a vocational and spiritual trajectory which is biblical, humanising and consistent with God's plan of salvation for all creation. It is the way of the cross. A way which descends deeply before it ascends. It is the way of the storm, the shipwreck, the belly of the whale, darkness and disappointment. A way which leads us into grace—not utility, or ambition or a need to succeed—but grace. Furthermore, this way leads us into grace not as a status but as a flow. Grace is not the end of the road. It is simply a new beginning. The way of the cross starts to shape our vocation anew as a new road begins to unfurl beneath our feet and we are liberated enough to take it. If we are not travelling the way of the cross, if we do not recognise its paradox, its anguish and yet its invitation into the boundless world of grace, we may want to ask what vocational journey we are on instead, and to what end it might lead us. We need to hear the truth of this vocational journey at this time and in this place of immense anxiety, challenge and transition and the perfectly formed book of Jonah seems to me a wondrous distillation of its mysterious truths.

1

Journeying with ambition

Do you want to rise?
Begin by descending.
AUGUSTINE[1]

Now the word of the Lord came to Jonah the son of Amittai,
saying, 'Arise, go to Nineveh, that great city, and call out against
it, for their evil has come up before me.' But Jonah rose to flee
to Tarshish from the presence of the Lord.

JONAH 1:1–3A (ESV)

The book of Jonah opens with what appears to be the classic formula
for a book of prophecy: 'the word of the Lord came to...' Seeing it
nestled among the other minor prophets, you might be forgiven for
settling into a predictable expectation of what is to come. Except
that one word, the first word, translated 'now', is the writer's way of
indicating that this book is of another genre altogether. For this little
Hebrew word is the typical introduction to a story, a narrative. It is the
equivalent of our 'once upon a time'. It is that concise way of making
sure we know that what comes next is a story that has something to
teach us.

Immediately, as in all good stories, tension is created, and along with
tension, questions. What will happen to Nineveh? What will happen to
Jonah? And will there be a connection? How is this tension between
the word of God and the will of his prophet going to be resolved?
We might also ask, what is going on inside Jonah? Why does Jonah
reject God's call to preach in Nineveh? The writer of Jonah does not
tell us. However, we do know a little of Jonah's background, enabling
us to make a guess. The rest of the story reveals quite a lot about
Jonah's inner self, allowing us to debate whether that guess might be
somewhere near the truth.

There is another reference to Jonah in the Old Testament that provides
an intriguing context to the story. In 2 Kings we are told that Jeroboam

II's reign over the Northern Kingdom of Israel was a prosperous one. We are told that he 'restored the boundaries of Israel' (14:25). Territory lost to the Assyrians was regained and for a brief period Israel's territorial sovereignty was restored (14:25a, 28). In the broader context of the time, with Israel and Judah surrounded by larger and more powerful kingdoms (Egypt, Assyria and Babylon), this was a remarkable turn of events. So it is with some significance that we are told that all this took place 'in accordance with the word of the Lord, the God of Israel, spoken through his servant Jonah son of Amittai' (14:25b).

How might we imagine Jonah at the opening of the story? Undoubtedly he is a 'successful' prophet. He has had the ear of the king, Jeroboam II, during a time of remarkable success that has gone against the grain of the history of the time. Jeroboam II is certainly no righteous king. He is straight out of the mould of the first king of Israel, Jeroboam son of Nebat, whose story is told in 1 Kings 11:26—15:30. It is a story of rebellion, deception, cruelty and idolatry. A reign deliberately calculating in its desire for power and authority, which begins by distinguishing clearly and dramatically the alternative rule he is offering by establishing alternative gods for the people of Israel to worship. This pattern of authoritarian rule, underpinned by false gods and war with Judah, continues into the time of Jeroboam II.

The mention of 'the word of the Lord, the God of Israel' (2 Kings 14:25) in this context then is a rare in-breaking of God's voice into an atmosphere in which this might well have been politically seditious. Jonah must have been brave. He may well also have been something of a gifted politician, learning to play the game and speak the language that enabled him to have the ear of the king and keep it. Jeroboam was unlikely to be particularly interested in the source of Jonah's advice. More likely he was simply interested in Jonah getting it right. Which he did. So Jonah's star rose and rose as he became one of the king's most important and trusted military and political advisers.

This should not mean that we start to see Jonah as nothing more than a political adviser. The writer of 2 Kings is striking a note of hope, inserting a detail of profound theology within what is a rather bleak and pessimistic narrative. God has not given up on rebellious, idolatrous Israel (14:27) and has not left his people without witness and without hope. Jonah represents a small but insistent voice of salvation in the midst of the wreckage resulting from the hubris of Jeroboam I and his descendants.

However, what this man of God has experienced, in the tough and devious corridors of power in Israel, is success. A success that must be in no small measure down to his own abilities and strength of character. Furthermore, that success may not have been a result of the king's sympathy with his gift as a prophet. Jonah is probably only as good as his next prophecy. The cruel mathematics of political expediency surely suggest that prophecies of doom, or prophecies that prove to be plain wrong, are hardly likely to extend Jonah's career; on the contrary, they would bring it to a rather abrupt end.

And so it is in this context that the 'word of the Lord came to Jonah… "Go to Nineveh, that great city, and call out against it"' (Jonah 1:1–2, ESV). Jonah knows the Lord, he hears the word of God—this is his undoubted gift. He has served God faithfully and courageously by bravely speaking the word of God to a hostile audience. It has brought him success and favour. It has almost certainly brought him prosperity and safety within the paranoid and ruthless world of the Jeroboams. And so with this new word from God Jonah is brought to a crossroads. Nineveh, capital of the Assyrian empire, is the seat of power of one of Israel's key enemies. It is from this locus of power that Israel has seen significant gain. But it is also a continued threat. Asking the king for permission to go to Nineveh to preach 'the word of the Lord' might well have been interpreted by Jeroboam II as subterfuge and treason. So perhaps for this reason Jonah loses his nerve. He cannot see a way out—he knows he should obey what God is saying to him, but he also knows that in obeying he is likely to lose everything: status, significance, career, security and perhaps even life itself.

Jonah may well fear for his own personal security in the face of an unpredictable king, and he may fear losing much else besides. Speaking God's word as political advice has brought Jonah significance and security. It is easy to imagine how that begins to distort things. God himself so easily becomes a mere adjunct to the work of providing divinely inspired advice to the king. God becomes the source of Jonah's success. And with all that success perhaps God easily becomes nothing more than a facility, a utility. Consequently, Jonah begins to see himself as the chief architect of this success, with God as some kind of talisman, giving his blessing, his spiritual stamp of authority on Jonah's wisdom and advice. Jonah is at the helm of his own enterprise, with God delegated to the role of chief adviser. God is being imported into the realm of Jonah's ambition.

However, when we have learnt to utilise God for our own ambitions, a considerable dilemma comes when his ambition for us, his call on our life, presents us with a challenge beyond our own ability. There really is nowhere to go when God's ambition for us asks more of us than we can imagine shouldering.

So, as I read the book of Jonah, a book that constantly raises questions and never really answers them, a book that appears to point questions at Jonah but is really pointing questions at us, I ended up asking myself a key question. What is ambition? More specifically, what is godly ambition? Where is the place of ambition within a vocation? Where is the place of ambition within ministry? Within leadership? Is ambition good? Can it be good? When ministry and our own ambition meet, does the situation become something of a 'graveyard of ambition'? Can we resurrect ambition, sanctify it and allow it to serve us rather than master us? If so, how?

Ambition in creation

To explore a theology of ambition we might start at the beginning. Both creation accounts (Genesis 1 and 2) describe God bestowing worth and dignity on humankind through the delegation of a role and a task of work. It is clear that God has made us to be useful. We are asked to 'rule over the fish in the sea and the birds in the sky and over every living creature that moves on the ground' (Genesis 1:28). Similarly, we are told that 'The Lord God took the man and put him in the Garden of Eden to work it and take care of it' (2:15). As human beings we are not simply spectators of God's creation, passive observers with nothing more to do than wonder at and appreciate the work of another. We are invited to take part in the ongoing work and stewarding of creation. We are offered lives of meaning and purpose, lives that promise profound significance.

This is part of our nature. No wonder we seek it. We seek significance, meaning and purpose. We seek meaningful and purposeful work precisely because that is how we are created to be. We are ambitious for it, it is in our nature to achieve it. We have work to do. And, made in the image of God, we naturally desire that work to be 'good'. In this is the root of ambition. So ambition is a good thing, having its origins in a good God.

Of course, there are two accounts of creation and these may well point to a dual nature of human beings.[2] The two Adams of these creation accounts—'Adam the first' and 'Adam the second'—are different. Adam the first is charged with the imperative to 'fill the earth and subdue it. Rule over… every living creature that moves on the ground' (Genesis 1:28). This first Adam is thus essentially utilitarian in nature, looking at creation and asking, 'How?' 'How can I subdue?' 'How can I create?' 'How can I succeed?' His default response to God's charge is to use his intellect and ingenuity to solve, create, subdue and dominate. The development of this Adam's mode of being in community is a community of great achievement, immense resourcefulness and ingenuity, a 'majestic community'.[3]

Adam the second, however, is first of all formed 'from the dust of the ground' (Genesis 2:7) and then put in the Garden of Eden by God 'to work it and take care of it' (v. 15). This creation narrative focuses on the importance of relationship. God says, 'It is not good for the man to be alone' (v. 18) and so creates a companion for him. Adam the second's mode of being is one of service and relationship. His key question is not so much 'How?' but 'Why?' 'Why am I here?' 'Why am I lonely?' But he also asks, 'Who?' 'Who is this presence that seems to follow me?' 'Who is the person who can fulfil my need for relationship, for unity, for reciprocal love?' Adam's response to the world around him is one of humble service and sacrifice in search of fulfilment. The community he creates is one of mutuality, common good and harmony—a 'covenantal community'.[4]

Neither Adam, however, is more moral or desirable than the other. This is the point, that both are part of how we were created. But they do live in apparent contradiction to one another. We are driven to create, to subdue, to use our intellect and ingenuity in the use of the materials we find around us in creation. We often call this ambition. However, we are also created to serve, to surrender, to relate, to offer something of that same self in sacrifice to the wider good, the broader community. This creates a fundamental confrontation between the utilitarian logic of Adam the first and the inverse logic of serving, sacrificing Adam the second. As *New York Times* columnist David Brooks has observed, 'To nurture your Adam I career, it makes sense to cultivate your strengths. To nurture your Adam II moral core, it is necessary to confront your weaknesses.'[5]

That confrontation is at the very heart of the dilemma we face when we talk of ambition. We are right to question the strident ambition depicted by Adam the first. While it is good, we are conscious of its potential for overreaching itself. In alliance with the ego in each one of us, ambition has the power to turn itself from a servant into a master. This is the root of all idolatry. Making that which was made to serve humankind into a master. We could say, 'Ambition was made for man, not man for ambition' (compare Mark 2:27).

Ambition needs rescuing and putting in its proper context so that it may become good again. Ambition needs to find its way beyond the confrontation between Adam the first and Adam the second and enter into the more covenantal world that seeks relationship with oneself, with others, with creation and with God. We do not have to dump ambition at the threshold between one and the other; rather ambition begins to take on a more mature form, still benefiting from the drive of the charge to subdue and create, but transformed and redeemed by a deeper call to serve and offer one's gifts and talents in the service of others.

The language of ambition

Language provides another way of helping us explore this. The word 'love' is fundamental to understanding God, the gospel and our relationship with God and one another. It is a word that, in contrast to the biblical languages, does double, if not triple, duty in the English language. Pope Benedict XVI writes that 'love' has become one of the most frequently used and misused words, a word to which we attach different meanings.[6] In particular, he argues that one use of that word 'love'—'love between a man and a woman, where body and soul are joined together and human beings glimpse an apparently irresistible promise of happiness'—has become in our day the 'epitome of love' to which all other kinds and meanings of love are pale comparisons.[7]

The biblical languages have various words to denote different types of love. Hebrew has two words. *Dodim* refers to a love that is insecure, uncertain and which is still searching, on a quest. This then transforms into *ahaba* (the Hebrew form of the Greek *agape*), which denotes a love that involves a real discovery of another and a willingness to rescind selfishness and seek the good of another at personal expense to oneself. The Greek *philia* describes the love of friendship and *agape* the love which prefers the other in a way that is sacrificial of the self. Though not used in the New Testament, Greek also has the word *eros*, which refers to that passionate, unwilled love between a man and a woman.

Dodim and *ahaba*, *eros* and *agape* express something towards a better understanding of what it is to love and for our expression of love to mature from selfish desire into selfless service of others. *Eros* has been described as 'ascending' love, love which reaches out for more, for the ecstatic, for satisfaction. *Agape*, by contrast, is 'descending' love characterised by being grounded in service, faith and the letting fall of those desires for self. However, the two are not opposites; *eros* is not discarded but rather enters into the wider scope of *agape*. We don't stop desiring and needing love. Instead those desires and needs are taken up by the greater concerns of *agape* love. So Pope Benedict concludes, '*Eros* is thus supremely ennobled, yet at the same time it is so purified as to become one with *agape*.'[8]

The same then can be said of ambition, which is after all a subset of love, a desire within the panoply of desires which make up our essential desire for significance, love and acceptance. Perhaps our lack of confidence with the word 'ambition'—which can lead to false humility, a product of the pushing down of all ambition—is because we have lost sight of the distinctions between different forms of ambition. If raw ambition is the equivalent of *eros*, then there is nothing intrinsically wrong with it; it is part of how we were created and something to be nurtured. However, original ambition is 'ascending ambition', which left unchecked seeks ascendancy, a god status in our lives. Like *eros*, it needs disciplining, ennobling and transforming within the wider scope of 'descending ambition', an ambition which has been taken up and taken in—into the concerns and desires of God, for his kingdom and his creation.

So in understanding ambition as having these two related forms, or phases, it may help to distinguish one from the other. To do that, the word we might use for 'descending ambition' is 'vocation'. Vocation, from the Latin *vocare*, to call, captures that sense of God calling us beyond ourselves and into self-giving, into a purpose we feel created and shaped for. Vocation is therefore the maturing of our desires for status and purpose, the maturing of ambition. So as God seeks to nurture the desires of ambition in us, he is not wanting to stamp out such desires as though they were dirty, unhealthy things. But he is deeply interested in calling those desires into the scope of his ambitions, his love, his sovereign plans. This requires a descent on our part, a losing of oneself in order to find oneself. This is precisely what Jesus was talking about when he said, 'Whoever tries to keep their life will lose it, and whoever loses their life will preserve it' (Luke 17:33). The paradoxical truth is that when we cease allowing ambition to drive us, while it feels like losing life, losing control, losing significance and purpose, it is in fact a journey on, a journey down and then up, a transcendence towards a higher ambition as our ambition is taken up into the purposes for which it was made—our vocation.

The ambition of Jesus

When we recognise the deeper truth of this paradoxical journey, we welcome the truth of the gospel into our vocation. For this is the way of Christ, the paradox of life lost to receive life gained. This is the way of the cross, a journey that to reach its ultimate goal will involve humiliation, the loss of all that we are, and ultimately death, before transcendence and transformation come in the form of resurrection. This journey is captured perfectly in the early church hymn of Philippians 2.

> In your relationships with one another, have the same mindset
> as Christ Jesus:
> who, being in very nature God,
> did not consider equality with God something to be used to his
>   own advantage;
> rather, he made himself nothing
> by taking the very nature of a servant,
> being made in human likeness.
> And being found in appearance as a man,
> he humbled himself
> by becoming obedient to death—
> even death on a cross!
> Therefore God exalted him to the highest place
> and gave him the name that is above every name,

that at the name of Jesus every knee should bow,
in heaven and on earth and under the earth,
and every tongue acknowledge that Jesus Christ is Lord,
to the glory of God the Father.
PHILIPPIANS 2:5–11

Jesus models the vocational journey. The awesome creativity and ingenuity of our ambition, without being confronted, transformed and ennobled by our more relational, sacrificial nature, can tempt us towards 'equality with God'. Jesus chooses to let go of that equality and models a life of service and sacrifice. He is confronting precisely the contradiction in our nature that the two creation accounts point to. He chooses servanthood and he accepts the humility of suffering and death because to be fully human is to offer our very nature, with all its God-given gifts, to others. This is Adam the second's nature. This is descendent ambition. Jesus' descendent journey is transformed into one of exaltation as he is lifted once again 'to the highest place' (v. 9) and given the position of ultimate honour, where all humanity will come to acknowledge that he is Lord (vv. 10–11).

The journey from ambition to vocation begins with letting go. There is a distinct change of direction, a definite change of gear, when we begin to walk in vocation rather than ambition. Ambition is largely self-driven. We are motivated by something within us, something we struggle perhaps to articulate; it feels like something we must do, something that feels at first exciting and all-consuming. We are the ones pushing and urging ourselves on to achieve better and greater things.

The second part of the journey is different. The energy for the journey comes from somewhere else. It comes from outside ourselves. We choose to lose ourselves, lay down our agendas and our goals and listen to a different voice. We respond to the voice of God's calling even when it will call us beyond ourselves. This call at the same time draws on the material which has been driving us on so far, our natural gifts, talents and desires. Again, the call of God, our true vocation, is not something disconnected or different from our ambition. Rather, it is an ennobling, a purifying, a transformation of our created qualities: our gifts, talents, abilities, character. If we let him, God will take these up and use them creatively in the fulfilment of his own ambitions. Vocation then is ambition ennobled.

Our journey with ambition

The story of Jonah begins with a confrontation between ambition and vocation, between Adam the first and Adam the second. Jonah's successful career as political adviser, which has brought him so much significance and status precisely because he has been listening intently to the voice of God, is called upwards and onwards. Those gifts and experience, developed in one context, are now being called upon for another. But in order for Jonah to advance beyond ambition to vocation, from ascending ambition to descending ambition, something dramatic has to happen. The ego will not give up easily and the only way that its grasp on equality can be weakened is by challenging that presumption, that it has equality with God. To challenge that presumption, that illusion, in Jonah God calls him beyond the limits of his own resources. Those momentous opening words, 'Go to Nineveh, that great city, and call out against it' (Jonah 1:2, ESV), represent so much more than the standard call of a prophet to a new mission. This is the call of God to change Jonah into someone he would never otherwise have been.

What follows is a journey of descent, which is in fact the beginning of a journey of ascent, as Jonah's ambition, grasp of status and understanding of God are challenged and transformed. No doubt as for many of us, Jonah's understanding of God is right in theory. After all, he confesses that he knew that God is a 'gracious and compassionate God, slow to anger and abounding in love' (4:2). However, he has placed the ultimate sovereignty of God outside the orbit of his ambition, outside the orbit of his own personal security and status, a place where it could not remain without conflict.

Jonah's story reflects our own confusion on the subject of ambition. After all, much of Jonah's life and career looked pretty good, at least on the outside. I think we are struggling with a theology of ambition. Partly, I think this is because we have not recognised the distinction between ascending and descending ambition. We want to embrace ambition because it is a drive within us that has the potential for so much good. And yet, perhaps, we are scared of it because we see its potential to consume us in ways that are not good at all.

The word vocation certainly helps us reframe ambition as ambition is taken up into vocation and ennobled by it. Yet even the word vocation has its problems. It has been devalued by our religious institutions over the centuries by its narrow reference to those getting ordained, taking holy orders or working towards a licensed ministry within the Church. Somehow we need to free vocation to fulfil its ability to illustrate something critical about human flourishing. Vocation is not just about pursuing a certain career, perhaps one that is a bit more clearly service-oriented than others. It is about what it means to be human. We need to elevate vocation as a universal value which we all aspire to and encourage in ourselves and in others.

I often ask people, in some cases people who have been in good jobs for many years, what they feel called to do, what their vocation might be. Many respond with blank looks and say that no one has ever asked them that before! Yet it is not just ministers of one kind or another who are placed in Eden with something specific to do. It is part of our God-given nature to want to make a difference. And it is part of God's nature to want to shape that ambition into a vocation, out of his specific love for each one of us. A journey from ambition to vocation is, I believe, part of what it means to be human.

At root, our vocation begins with a calling made to us to follow in obedience, and to trust that in that following we are entrusting ourselves to the only real source of human flourishing. The archetype of vocation is Abraham, who apparently out of nowhere is called by a mysterious voice and asked to 'Go from your country, your people and your father's household to the land I will show you' (Genesis 12:1). What will be the result of obedience to this call? That God will bless Abraham and enable him and his family to flourish. Vocation is not ultimately about doing anything except listening to the voice of God and being obedient to it. And fundamentally vocation is a call into relationship with this God, trusting him as the source of our own flourishing.

And yet, as I have already said, that same calling will invite us to take action. It will invite us to participate in the creating and saving work of God. The remarkable thing is that both our flourishing and our action, both our being and our doing, find in our vocation a context for development. The specific miracle of our calling is that it will offer us purpose, meaningful work and action, but not without shaping our character and our soul. Our call is just as much about who we become as what we do. When we forget this we easily reduce our understanding of vocation to simply doing certain things for God, worse still to a role we carry out in some vaguely sacrificial, servant kind of way. God's ambition, his desire for us, is to lead us deeper into relationship with him, to transform us more and more into the likeness of Christ. One of the primary means by which he achieves this is by calling us into meaningful action with him.

Vocation in an ambitious society

Ambition's ability to overreach itself can also infect organisations and cultures. We live in a highly competitive, ambitious and managerial culture. It is a culture which is increasingly driven by a 'utilitarian calculus'.[9] Everything is becoming oriented towards success, achievement and productivity, while the challenges of the inner life, of developing character, facing our limitations, our mortality, and growing spiritually, have little currency. A few years ago, as a young curate, I went to a secondary school in Easter week to speak about the message of Easter. The sea of faces in front of me that day were all Year 11s, and all a few weeks from the beginning of their GCSE exams. I showed some film clips and talked about the resurrection, about Jesus rising from the dead and what it meant to me, how this event had shaped my life and how it gave me hope. When I finished, the Head of Year got up and spoke. I stood to one side expecting a few notices and bits of school administration. Instead he rather abruptly pointed at me and said, 'You see Vicar Paul there, he's a success!' That was not something I had expected to hear that morning! People don't tend to see ordained ministers as a 'success'! But he insisted, with some conviction, that this was the case. The gist of his slightly desperate message was that I was a model of success, I'd worked hard to get where I was, and if they wanted to be successful they needed to work hard and get decent grades in their GCSEs! I didn't necessarily disagree with his message. And I didn't feel uncomfortable being an illustration for it! But as I reflected on this event I realised something about it had really unsettled me. It was that the spiritual message that I had offered that morning had seemingly been ignored, not so much because it was Christian, or seen as irrelevant and mythical, but because it did not fit into a narrative that focused only on working hard in order to be successful in the future. There didn't seem space in that school for questioning what kind of human beings we might become—all the attention was given to what we might end up doing.

Vocation in this kind of culture is a real challenge. Giving people freedom to work out their vocation in arenas like education or medicine is massively challenged by a culture of competition that fosters a relentless drive for results and a plethora of targets set by distant managers. I think of a GP I know who retired early because he was told he had to see patients in less than ten minutes, when his deeply felt vocation argued for the need for him to listen enough to each patient to really hear them and diagnose their ailment. I think of the community of monks I have recently returned from whose vocation as an educational establishment has altered radically in the last generation as professionalisation and managerialism in the education sector has increased.

Sadly, the Church is not immune to this cultural assault. We talk of vocation, yet the pressure for results, the thirst for data, the plethora of models and programmes and five-year plans all speak of an organisation whose trust in the call of God on those who are working out their vocation as ministers in the Church is increasingly tempered by anxious managerialism. We believe in giving people freedom to follow God in the place and time in which they are, but when 'growth' has permeated our language and our vision so thoroughly, the tendency to manage, to impose, to control begins to take hold.

Pioneer missionaries can find themselves at the sharp end of that experience. Often under pressure, in situations of time-limited sources of funding, with an urgency to reach sustainability in unrealistic timeframes, they find the freedom to work out their vocation can be massively compromised by the need for quick results. It concerns me that such an environment will cause many pioneers to act hastily, roll out the programmes and the courses, the models and the ministries, and never make the journey from ambition to vocation. Taking that road is likely to lead to burnout, disappointment and the disappearance of individuals with the sort of apostolic vocation the Church acutely needs.

To journey from ambition to vocation, allowing our ascending ambition to be shaped into the descending ambition of the gospel, requires two things that the book of Jonah is full of—a raw encounter with our inner self, and a raw encounter with the person of God. This cannot be manufactured. It starts with letting go and continues through the kind of adventure that will employ ships, storms, whales, foreign lands and outlandish assignments. We will have our own equivalents, all as surprising and unlikely as those of Jonah when we reflect on them. The point is that it will take us beyond ourselves in a way that all the pretty models and programmes never will because such approaches rarely take us beyond the remit of our own control.

Furthermore, the busyness that these approaches inevitably create detracts from the things we desperately need: space to encounter our inner self and space to encounter God. Our busyness blinds us to the storm that is growing around us and inside us. Something dramatic is required to make us face up to the reality of ourselves and the direction in which we are travelling. The idol of our own ambition, expressed in works of great importance that fill our diaries and our lives, has to be knocked out of centre. Then and only then can the painful but beautiful work begin of transforming ambition, taking it up, ennobling it, letting it die and rise again as a nascent vocation.

2
Taking flight

Do not go to another place, it will do you a great deal of harm.
AMMA SYNCLETICA[10]

But Jonah ran away from the Lord and headed for Tarshish. He went down to Joppa, where he found a ship bound for that port. After paying the fare, he went aboard and sailed for Tarshish to flee from the Lord.
JONAH 1:3

Who of us hasn't run away from someone or something at some point? And for all sorts of reasons. Some understandable. Some irresponsible. Some a mixture of both. We are primed to respond to pressure and danger in one of two ways—fight or flight. We do a lot of both as we grow up, but gradually our experience and maturity grow to the point where all but the most serious of dangers and pressures override our will and our reason most of the time.

There does seem a mixture of reason and panic in Jonah's response to the call of God. He is rational enough to form a plan, think of a place as far away as possible (and yet reachable) and get there as quickly as possible. Tarshish fits the bill perfectly.

No one really knows where Tarshish was, though it most certainly was a real place, rather than a metaphorical or imaginary one. Some scholars have located Tarshish on the southern tip of India, others on the tip of the Iberian Peninsula. Its location, however, is not the real issue. The real issue is what Tarshish represents. It was a place known for its shipping. Trading ships came to Joppa laden with silver and ore and other natural resources. It was clearly a great distance away, requiring a lengthy sea crossing. For Jonah, Tarshish perhaps represents 'far, far away', a kind of fairy tale place of abundance. It also represents somewhere on the edge of nowhere, somewhere virtually unreachable, somewhere escapist. It is somewhere where Jonah could escape all his responsibilities, to Jeroboam and to God.

What is Tarshish?... In the story it is anywhere—anywhere but the right place; it is the opposite direction, the direction a person takes when he turns his back on his destiny... It is the excuse we give... our rationalisations.[11]

But for all his rationalisations Jonah is clearly gripped by something fairly irrational. Does he really believe that Yahweh, creator of the universe, can be outwitted by Jonah taking the first ship out of town? Readers of the story would know that running away from the Lord's presence was simply not possible. They would immediately think of Psalm 139, with its questions:

> *Where can I go from your Spirit?*
> *Where can I flee from your presence?*
> **PSALM 139:7**

The psalmist asserts:

> *If I settle on the far side of the sea*
> *even there your hand will guide me,*
> *your right hand will hold me fast.*
> **PSALM 139: 9–10**

Jonah is no stranger to the psalms, as his prayer in chapter 4 will show us, much of which is drawn verbatim from the psalms (see, for example, Psalm 103:8). Does Jonah's conception of God really include limiting God in terms of time and space? There are clear signs of delusion here, of what modern psychologists might call cognitive dissonance. Jonah's actions do not match his fundamental beliefs. He is running scared, of God yes, but ultimately of what the call of God on his life is forcing him to confront.

The post office in Stornoway

Let's be honest, we all have a Tarshish. Maybe it's retirement. Maybe it's the life we might have had if things had turned out differently. Maybe it's the fulfilment of our ambition when work, life and ministry will reach some plateau of ease and success. Maybe it's the point of 'breakthrough' when all our hard work for God and his kingdom somehow is rewarded with fruitfulness. Or maybe it's simply that visceral desire to go somewhere, anywhere away from the heavy demands of responsibility that ministry, and particularly leadership, brings.

A beguiling poem called 'Swineherd' by Eiléan Ní Chuilleanáin captures it perfectly for me. It opens with the lines:

When all this is over, said the swineherd,
I mean to retire, where
Nobody will have heard of my special skills
And conversation is mainly about the weather.[12]

Work, even good work, places us within the expectations and demands of others. It places us within the realms of seriousness and responsibility. And at times the daily round of these responsibilities, of agendas and ambitions, of hopes and visions, becomes a burden we simply want to lay down. At times we long for it all to be over. At times we 'mean to retire'. We would give it all up for insignificance ('nobody will have heard of my special skills') and triviality ('conversation is mainly about the weather') if we could. And we begin to dream of doing so.

About four years into my time as a pioneer minister I began to suffer from a recurring vision that I struggled to shake off. In this vision, or fantasy more like, I was the manager of the post office at Stornoway in the Outer Hebrides. Running the post office there, I told myself, is a simple job with a neat beginning and end each day, limited and manageable responsibilities, plenty of simple doable tasks and lots of job satisfaction from doing logical tasks, ticking boxes, that sort of thing. And, of course, there is ample spare time to enjoy space, beauty and a simple life far away from the complexities of where I am right now. It's important to note that I have never been to Stornoway, or indeed to the

Outer Hebrides. No doubt if the manager of the post office in Stornoway is reading this they might want to get in touch and tell me what a hard and responsible job it is. But as with all fantasies, that is not the point. Indeed the point is precisely that, like Jonah's Tarshish, it is a place I have not been to and which I can therefore imagine to be a perfect escape from all that I want to be rid of in my present predicament. We don't create realistic fantasies. We create Utopian visions that feel like heaven, like the kind of life we are desperate to live, but are not earthed in a place of our own experience. Reality would confront us with the truth that relocating somewhere else, somewhere that seems idyllic, quiet, simple and undemanding, is not going to solve the dilemmas that we face. And that is precisely the truth we wish to avoid.

Eiléan Ní Chuilleanáin's poem 'Swineherd' continues to detail such a Utopia:

> I want to learn how to make coffee, at least as well
> As the Portuguese lay-sister in the kitchen
> And polish the brass fenders every day.
> I want to lie awake at night
> Listening to cream crawling to the top of the jug
> And the water lying soft in the cistern.
>
> I want to see an orchard where the trees grow in straight lines
> And the yellow fox finds shelter between the navy-blue trunks,
> Where it gets dark early in summer
> And the apple-blossom is allowed to wither on the bough.[13]

This is not a real vision—it borders on the delusional, with disparate, even surreal, details such as Portuguese lay-sisters, brass fenders and crawling cream, yellow foxes and early summer darkness. But the feel of it is beautiful, restful, intoxicating. No doubt Tarshish conjured up similar images for Jonah, images generated from stories and fables of this frontier port, images with a patina of truth but a core substance born of a desperate desire to escape the reality of his dilemma.

The post office in Stornoway was my Tarshish, somewhere that promised deliverance from all that was starting to trouble me in the place of my true calling. It was a flight of fancy, a flight from a growing responsibility I shouldered which was starting to feel too much. I only had to reflect on the nature of my personal Tarshish to begin to understand what it was about my own responsibilities I was seeking escape from. I was desperate for order, for work that had beginnings and ends, work that had achievable and measurable goals, work that offered a clear sense of achievement and satisfaction, and work that you could shut the door on and say goodbye to at the end of the day.

More than that though, my experience as a pioneer minister, nurturing emerging communities of disciples from nothing, was one of constant peril. Peril sounds a bit hyperbolic perhaps. But like the children's DVDs that bear warnings of 'mild peril', perhaps pioneer ministry should come with a warning of 'constant peril'! It is peril in the sense of a consistent feeling that all that has started to form, that is small, fragile, often chaotic, might disappear at any moment. You feel constantly at the mercy of circumstances beyond your control, with little or no tradition, little wider experience, and only a glimmer of what the future holds. The ground beneath your feet feels unstable and unreliable. The ground in front of you only emerges as you venture onto it one step at a time. It all sounds so glamorous and pioneering in a Wild West kind of way, but the experience of leading such a process with a community of people felt like carrying a precious vase across a marble floor—and the vase was covered in grease. Being in peril is exactly how it feels to be a pioneer.

Though, of course, this is how it is. Venturing into the unknown, beyond the prevailing structures and into territory that is uncertain and unmapped is precisely what brings about feelings of peril. We talk of the adventure of faith, sometimes selling discipleship and leadership as exciting and exhilarating. Yet we do not stop to fully take stock of what we mean when we use the word adventure. There is no adventure without danger. There is no adventure without peril, without uncertainty, without deep experiences of vulnerability and fear.

One only has to read Paul's second letter to the Corinthians to pick up the truth of this. In the letter, Paul lays bare the cost of his own adventure in following the call of Jesus into the unknown.

> I have worked much harder [than anyone else], been in prison more frequently, been flogged more severely, and been exposed to death again and again. Five times I received from the Jews the forty lashes minus one. Three times I was beaten with rods, once I was pelted with stones, three times I was shipwrecked, I spent a night and a day in the open sea, I have been constantly on the move. I have been in danger from rivers, in danger from bandits, in danger from my fellow Jews, in danger from Gentiles; in danger in the city, in danger in the country, in danger at sea; and in danger from false believers. I have laboured and toiled and have often gone without sleep; I have known hunger and thirst and have often gone without food; I have been cold and naked.
>
> 2 CORINTHIANS 11:23B–27

Yet, having listed such a crushing catalogue of physical suffering and psychological perils, he adds this final comment: 'Besides everything else, I face daily the pressure of my concern for all the churches' (11:28).

In the same category as the sort of suffering most of us would wince at, Paul puts the burden of responsibility for the churches he has planted. Daily, he faces that responsibility. Deprivations and physical sufferings come and go but the constant freight of love and care for the fledgling communities of new disciples across Turkey and Greece weighs heavily on him. When I read that in the midst of my own experience I felt the relief of knowing my feelings were understandable. Yet at the same time everything in me wanted to flee from all of it, to my vision of Utopia, where all was manageable, deliverable and reliable.

Relocation, relocation

If I wasn't dreaming of the Outer Hebrides, I was paying closer and closer attention to that other source of Utopian dreams and Tarshish fantasies—the job section of the *Church Times*. I felt guilty as I did. Flitting through the ads trying not to be too interested was like trying not to look at the calling cards stuck up in London telephone boxes. I knew what I was doing was not helping me, but I did it anyway.

We all know the game and play it regardless. Job adverts play on our fantasies, making much of the beautiful location, the substantial vicarage, the standard of the local schools. And we play the game of relocation, relocation, a gentle weekly perusal of back pages, with no harm done.

But, of course, it is harmful. It is harmful in the way that soft porn is harmful—seemingly innocuous but leading our desires elsewhere and making our real loves, our real commitments seem unsatisfactory. Spending time among the job adverts can be like popping into the travel agents just to browse. We aren't intending to book a holiday, but how can we not when the pictures promise so much and the costs seem so reasonable? The jobs section can be the travel agent to our dreams of Tarshish, offering tickets of escape for anyone willing to pay the price.

The relocation game is not new. Far from it. The monasteries of the early centuries of Christianity suffered from the same malaise. As the monastic movement expanded, new frontiers of monasticism opened up. As a result more choices opened up, a market for monks, who could be tempted to imagine that what really ailed and challenged them in their experience of monastic life could better be addressed by simply finding another monastery. St Benedict called them 'gyrovagues', literally 'circle wanderers', those on the move, but going nowhere. Augustine called them 'circumcellions', 'those who prowl around the barns', apparently circling at the peripheries, but never quite landing. They were monks that were almost continuously itinerant, looking for the community that might fit them, the colleagues that might prove more comfortable.

Amma Syncletica, a fourth-century desert mother, wrote advisedly: 'If you are living in a monastic community, do not go to another place, it will do you a great deal of harm.'[14] Clearly this was a considerable problem among these communities as they proliferated and grew. Eventually it took an intervention from St Benedict to try to put a stop to it. Benedict introduced a new vow—the vow of stability. A vow simply to stay put, a vow to resist the temptation to flee, a vow to stay and face those things that you are fleeing from, to learn from them and grow personally, to embrace them spiritually. 'To try to escape boredom, sexual frustration, restlessness, unsatisfied desire by searching for fresh tasks and fresh ideas,' writes Rowan Williams on this theme, 'is to attempt to seal off these areas from grace.'[15]

Clearly you do not have to be a monk to appreciate this tension and temptation. Vocation and ministry are the crucible in which our own frailties are exposed. When it gets tough doing the very thing we feel called to do, it is far easier to think of doing the same thing somewhere else than face the harsh truths within ourselves.

For those in leadership, there is the great danger of a flight into fantasy, a Tarshish of our imaginations that provides a convenient distraction from the inner challenges pushing up from below. Leadership can be like a huge screen onto which we and others project our greatest hopes and expectations. Vision is what, as leaders in mission, we are encouraged to create and communicate. But where does vision slide into fantasy? Where does it morph into self-justification? How do we prevent the projections and expectations of others, and of our own divided self, becoming the main image on the screen?

I am reminded of the 1939 film *The Wizard of Oz*, which tells of a man of great and wonderful reputation whom no one appears to have seen but who lives in a magical castle at the end of the yellow brick road. When Dorothy and her fellow travellers finally make their way there, they are confronted with a vision of smoke and light and noise, and a booming voice from within. Yet the wonderful Wizard of Oz is soon exposed as a rather small and feeble man simply turning the crank of this great machine. In an ecclesiastical context of great anxiety and uncertainty, where those in leadership can easily be exalted to the roles of saviour, magician and wizard, there is a road that leads to Oz. A place where we inflate numbers, exaggerate stories, play down failures and play up the future in order to distract ourselves from the voices that speak the unwelcome truth about ourselves.

In the same way, pioneer ministry creates a particular pressure to do this in an ecclesiastical environment of scarce resources and ongoing debate about the role and future of new forms of church. Most pioneer ministry projects begin with time-limited funding. Many begin with overly ambitious projections of when the project might become self-sustaining. From day one the pressure is on to grow a community large and committed enough to be financially sustainable. We are under pressure to fund ourselves and under pressure to prove ourselves. In such a climate the urge to be soothsayers, not prophets or apostles, is great. In such a climate, a flight from a calling that may be clear and significant becomes a pernicious temptation.

Flight towards oneself

Jonah's flight is a flight from his present location, but it is also a flight from the responsibility of obedience. There is an outer flight whose distance can be measured and direction plotted. But of most interest to the author of the story is the inner flight, the flight of Jonah from the challenge to himself.

God's call to 'Go', or in some translations 'Arise, go', is contrasted by the writer with words of descent. The call to Nineveh in the east sends Jonah heading west towards Joppa. The road to Joppa on the coast means he heads downward. And this downward trajectory is reiterated. After going down to Joppa, Jonah goes 'down into the inner part of the ship' (Jonah 1:5, ESV). After being called once again, this time by the ship's captain, to 'Arise' (1:6, ESV) he is eventually thrown into the sea and finally he goes down 'to the roots of the mountains' (2:6). Jonah's descent indicates 'how Jonah is totally separating himself from God, both horizontally (toward Tarshish) and vertically (toward the bottom of the sea)'.[16] Jonah's descent is not only a fact of geography—it is also personal and spiritual.

For the early desert fathers and mothers the sense of the word 'flight' was not a negative one. Abba Theodore of Pherme identified 'poverty, asceticism and flight'[17] as the three fundamental things necessary for life. As more and more people sought out this remote and isolated life in the Egyptian desert it might seem that the sense of this word 'flight' was of a flight away from human company, from civilisation, and towards the presence of God in the desert. However, it is more subtle than that. What these early monastic communities were encouraging flight from was the sort of environments that prevented people from facing up to their own sins, their own fragility and failure. They fled into the desert not to escape people but to face up to themselves in order that others might benefit more significantly. It was not flight *from* responsibility. Quite the opposite, it was flight *for the sake of* responsibility. It was avoiding precisely that temptation to solve your insecurities and crises of identity, either by surrounding yourself with projected images of success or by running off to the next place or assignment that might give you the fulfilment you so craved.

The commitment to flight consequently looked like staying put. It looked like 'sitting in your cell and weeping for your sins',[18] taking a long hard look at yourself with the help of God alone, fleeing the addictive habit of self-justification by any means and trying to retrain yourself in the way of God's gracious acceptance of who you are. Flight, in this context, is flight towards oneself, not in a self-serving way, but in a deeply responsible way that involves pain, suffering and sacrifice.

Few, if any, of us choose such a path proactively. Many of us avoid this path as long as possible. Indeed, psychologist Abraham Maslow coined the phrase 'Jonah syndrome' to refer to exactly that. He recognised in Jonah a human reaction when faced with the call to take responsibility. We know implicitly that responsibility is no easy ride. It will challenge us, confront us. It will involve pain, humiliation and personal exposure. For all the rewards it may offer, responsibility comes at a great cost. Maslow wrote:

> To discover in oneself a great talent certainly brings exhilaration but it also brings a fear of the dangers, responsibilities and duties of being a leader and of being alone. Responsibility can be seen as a heavy burden and evaded as long as possible.[19]

Vocation. Call. The invitation to take responsibility. The invitation to lead. All offer to us a way that we know will be tough. The way is laid open to us and we can choose to take it or not. Once on it, though, the choices do not end. Along its length are endless diversions and alternative routes that look like shortcuts or scenic, less demanding, routes to our destination. To flee to oneself is to resist the urge to choose easier ways. It is the choice again and again to embrace our call, our vocation, with all its pain, challenge and personal cost. Frequently it is the choice to stay put even when that feels like death.

Choosing to become

In choosing to flee to oneself, we choose God's invitation to become. The choice to flee to oneself is the choice to give oneself up to God's call to us, not just to go somewhere and do something for him, but to be the person God is helping us to become. Our vocation is not just about doing. Our vocation has very much to do with what we become. That seems precisely why in the course of following the way of our calling we will come up against something that is utterly beyond the limits of our own abilities and skills. We are confronted with the reality of our own smallness. Our skills and abilities have served us well until this point, but somehow we are now being called beyond the limits of their capacity. We are being led to the edge of our private resources and are having to learn that the origin and course of our vocation do not depend on our abilities but on the mind and power of God.

This is a hugely significant transition and one which we do not choose or engineer ourselves. Indeed perhaps we cannot, since 'any attempt to engineer or plan your own enlightenment will be doomed to failure because it will be ego driven'.[20] It is a transition from what feels like safety and security to what feels like chaos, uncertainty and fear. No wonder we fight it, no wonder we flee from it. We perform what Richard Rohr calls our 'survival dance' for a great deal of our lives, gaining important skills and resources along the way. But, ultimately, we are created to move beyond our survival dance and discover our 'sacred dance',[21] an experience of life and vocation where the lead dancer is no longer ourselves but God himself.

It is also a transition from one 'container' to another. Much of life is about establishing a platform, a container that gives us what we need to survive. But that is a means to an end. The end is to fulfil our calling. We need, as Archimedes said, 'both a lever and a place to stand'.[22] Creating a place to stand depends on a great number of things: family, institutions, traditions, values, employers. Then it depends on us to apply the resources and framework we have been given as we venture out into the world. But creating a lever, creating a true expression of our vocation, means going beyond hard work, diligence and the serious application of all that we have learnt, no matter how good and how strong. It means 'fleeing to oneself', facing up to our fear and vulnerability, facing up to the potential for failure, going beyond the limits of our own resourcefulness and beginning to draw faithfully and fundamentally on the resources of God.

Staying where you are is, therefore, often the step of obedience needed to make that transition. It is the deliberate choice, guided by God, to take the way that leads to personal discomfort, suffering, perhaps failure, because we acknowledge that our vocation is bound up with our becoming. Where we are might well be for us the equivalent of the Egyptian desert for the desert fathers and mothers, that place that every fibre of our being would rather flee from, but which we choose to inhabit. Where we are being called to, or having to stick with, might well be our very own Nineveh. It is fast becoming a task beyond us, in which we feel utterly alone, isolated, stripped of our securities and familiar patterns of technique and success. Yet if it is the place we are being called to 'arise and go to' it is surely the place where God would have us, not just to 'perform a task' or 'fulfil a role' but to allow him to continue the process of shaping us into the person we are, in him, becoming.

3

Falling into the storm

First there is the fall, then we recover from the fall. Both are the mercy of God!
JULIAN OF NORWICH[23]

Then the Lord sent a great wind on the sea, and such a violent storm arose that the ship threatened to break up.
JONAH 1:4

An oxymoron is a figure of speech that harbours an apparent contradiction: open secret, clearly confused, deafening silence. A few years after starting our ministry in Poole, those involved in the ministry created a charity to oversee the work that was beginning to emerge. The charity is called Poole Missional Communities and we invited Bishop Graham Cray, then leader of the Fresh Expressions national team, to come and speak at our launch. Before the service a group of us, including Bishop Graham, went for a meal. As we got up to leave, Bishop Graham moved over towards me and paused with the manner of someone who had something important to say. I shall never forget what he said: 'When I reflect on how to think about working with Fresh Expressions of church two words seem to capture it all—glorious chaos.'

Structures and containers

Glorious chaos. Glorious. Chaos. Those are two words that don't sit easily with one another. An oxymoron, surely, harbouring a pretty hefty contradiction. After all, nobody enjoys chaos. Few people choose it. We run from it instinctively. We much prefer form. We like structure. We like consistency. Structures like family, home, career, institutions, community, beliefs, values and identity give us a sense of safety, stability and control. They keep order in and chaos out. We work hard to create them and when they are threatened we will fight hard to preserve them. Rarely do we choose to break them up, sink them or voluntarily leave them. In fact such is our desire for comfort, safety and control that we might even rather die than be forced beyond these limits and into the unknown.

Structures and containers are something of a theme in the story of Jonah. You could see the story as one of Jonah moving through a series of 'forms': his life in Israel, the ship, the great fish, Nineveh, the booth around which the vine grows in the final chapter. As we learnt in the first chapter of this book, we can begin to see the kind of structure that Jonah had been able to create as top prophet in the court of Jeroboam II. That structure was blown apart the moment God asked him to go and preach to the Ninevites. Jonah runs down to Joppa and rather desperately places his trust in another structure, another container: a ship bound for Tarshish.

Anyone who goes to sea, even today, knows what uncertain and fragile structures ships are in the face of the power of the sea. Ancient cultures had a strong and healthy fear of the sea. Hebrew culture shares this understandable fear. In Hebrew literature the sea symbolises all that is chaotic and formless. It is a place full of monsters, myth and mystery. This is territory far from the presence of God, for God is a God of order and stability, land and structure.

So there is heavy irony in what happens next. For it is from the sea that God makes his next move. It is God who 'hurled a great wind upon the sea' (Jonah 1:4, ESV). This place of chaos and uncertainty is made even more chaotic, even more uncertain, by the hand of God. The place of fear and formlessness, where God is not supposed to be, is the locus for God's initiative and God's involvement in the unfolding drama of Jonah's life.

Sometimes our 'forms' prejudice us and blind us to the possibilities of God's presence and God's action. The faith we place in the structures of our lives, structures that have the provision of God written all over them, can so easily slip into a dogma that says this is the *only* place where God can be and God can work. We slip into simple distinctions where we define the boundaries between good and evil, light and darkness, presence and absence, order and chaos. But, in reality, we have created a religious form whose own survival is now dependent on these strict definitions. This is no longer about life. It is more about survival. So we cling to the forms that have served us well, even if those forms may not have a future or even when we are being asked to leave one form and find another.

I chose to leave what felt like a safe structure provided by traditional parish ministry in order to pursue what I perceived as a clear call to pioneer something new within the Church. One of the gifts of pioneers is that they can live lightly to structure. They are open to new forms, open to living without form at all. They are easily dissatisfied with the limitations of structures that are beginning to show signs of leakage or which seem no longer fit for purpose in many contexts.

Yet in the early days of my time as a pioneer minister I felt the loss of form keenly. The distinction is not between form and formlessness so much as between form and chaos. And chaos is not a pleasant feeling when you are exposed to it for too long. I longed for a dose of structure; like a drowning man hoping to cling on to a piece of floating debris, driftwood, anything, I craved something solid in the midst of all that was liquid. I would have gladly taken a funeral in those days. A nice, easy, simple funeral, of a well-loved, elderly relative who had lived a good life. I could do that well. It would have a beginning and an end and the family would appreciate me for it. Instead all around me was chaos, a diverse and bewildering community which offered few touchpoints, few foundations on which to build. All around me was chaos. And it was anything but glorious.

On the edge of chaos

And yet it is God who initiates a process of rising chaos and panic by creating the storm that engulfs Jonah's boat. The sailors do what sailors are paid to do and save the ship from breaking up. They lighten its load

(Jonah 1:5), they row for land (1:13). They also pray. These pagan sailors lead the way in recognising the limitations of the form to which they and Jonah have committed themselves. They are not foolish enough to go on fighting for this structure when it is clear that it is meeting with forces it is not capable of withstanding. So they pray and the captain wakes Jonah from his sleep in the depths of the ship and urges him to do the same. Why is Jonah asleep? Is it the sleep of faith? Faith in the ship? In the captain and crew? In God? More likely it is simply the action of an exhausted man who is desperate to get as far away from God and his call as possible. On the face of it, hiding from God in the darkness of a ship's hold, at sea, amid a bunch of heathen sailors, would seem like a good strategy. But that is the point. God does not conform to the containers we create for him. And from time to time he bursts out from the structures of our imaginations, our limitations and our expectations and speaks to us in ways that bring our cherished structures tumbling down. So it is that God's hand is in the gathering storm. God's voice comes in the guise of a pagan sailor reiterating the words of God that sent Jonah running in the opposite direction in the first place—'Arise!' (v. 6, ESV).

Chaos is full of potential for the glory of God. Chaos is not the place where God is not, a place we feel we have therefore to fill with the monsters and mysteries of our own imaginations. Chaos is perhaps more truly that place where God is in ways I have not understood, in ways that I do not have the form for, the structure, the language. We live, minister and explore our calling not in safety or structure but always on the edge between order and chaos. Order and chaos, light and darkness, presence and absence are not opposites to maintain but a dynamic to embrace. In rejecting chaos in favour of safety and predictability we close ourselves off from a vibrant synergy and creativity that is God's means of shaping us and how we are used.

One way in which we have experienced this dynamic is in the life of Reconnect, the missional community we planted in Poole. We were very deliberately committed to a life together of meeting and gathering that used places and spaces that were flexible and to some extent vulnerable. We felt that to be God's people was to be a people on the move, to be nomadic and open to the Spirit, open to where God would take us, trusting that this would be a key to our mission and ministry together. In this way we were welcomed in to use a first-floor room above a café in Poole High Street. Over time our little community grew through the use of this space and it quickly became a locus for meetings and one-to-one conversations, events in the evening, and a new community gathering around textile art during the week. Then on two separate occasions the use of that space was taken from us. In the first instance a change of management at the café led to an uncertain period where we initially assumed we would have to move on. We were thrown into chaos. Where would we meet? How would we meet? How could we meet anywhere except this place? Surely this was *the* place? On that occasion the new manager was open to negotiation and eventually agreed to us continuing to use this space. But the uncertainty, as we looked over the edge of safety and saw the waves and the growing storm, brought us back to God, reminded us that to be a nomadic community was to be a community deeply dependent on God and his guiding Spirit. Then nearly four years later we lost this space altogether. By then we had been running the café ourselves for three years. It had become our place and we loved it. We had become even more embedded, physically, emotionally and spiritually, in this place and yet we had to move on. Thankfully we had learnt. Not that it made it any easier. We gathered in prayer and we waited on God's Spirit. For the communities that had grown and developed in the four years we had been at the café, new venues and places of hospitality emerged to welcome us, and the life and growth of these communities has continued.

Transformation, of our communities and of ourselves, takes place in the dynamic between order and chaos. God sends the storm. God speaks through people who do not profess to speak for him. Chaos is not Godless or void but full of the potential for God to act and speak in the most creative and exciting ways. God is not exclusively a God of order, nor of chaos—he seems to do some of his best work at the boundary of the two.

Beginning to rise

As chaos threatens to engulf the ship, along with its crew and a sleeping prophet, Jonah is brought before the sailors, who question who on earth he is. The way the story is formed is important at this point. In Western literature we expect the key moment, the punchline of a story, to happen at the end. In Hebrew literature this takes place at the centre, at the hinge point of the story. This section has a characteristic symmetrical structure, mirroring a pattern of detail and development around a reflection point at the centre of the section. This pattern can be illustrated like this:

  A Introduction—Jonah flees the Lord (Jonah 1:3)
    B The Lord hurls the storm (1:4)
      C Sailors pray and act (1:5a, b)
        D Jonah acts (1:5c)
          E Sailors question Jonah (1:6–8)
            F *Jonah speaks (1:9)*
          E' Sailors question Jonah (1:10–11)
        D' Jonah responds (1:12)
      C' Sailors act (1:13–14)
    B' Sailors hurl Jonah, the storm ends (1:15)
  A' Conclusion—the sailors fear the Lord (1:16).[24]

The key moment, the punchline of the story, comes when Jonah speaks his first words. These words are responses to searching questions from the sailors. They are questions that go to the heart of the issue for the disobedient prophet. For while, in one sense, his predicament is a result of running away, paying a fare and committing himself to this ship on its passage across the sea, it is primarily an issue of a growing chaos around his true identity. Who is Jonah? He is Jonah, son of Amittai, a prophet in the court of the king of the Northern Kingdom of Israel. But beneath all of that, who is Jonah?

Jonah's names certainly give us some idea of who he is. Jonah means 'dove', which itself is a symbol of Israel. Amittai means 'faithfulness'. So this is Jonah, symbol of God's people, son of faithfulness. Quite a name to live up to! And, as ever with the writer of Jonah, there is irony in the expression of Jonah's name as the story unfolds and Jonah's actions contradict all that his name represents.

Furthermore, Jonah's identity is also heavily associated with boundaries. As we discovered, Jonah's prophecy is associated with a time when the boundaries of Israel were restored. Jonah's ministry appears to have helped affirm and strengthen Israel's sense of its own identity, which had been under considerable threat from the Assyrians. However, other prophets of the time, notably Amos, were not content with any complacency. Jonah and Jeroboam II may have restored physical boundaries but the soul of Israel as a nation was still under threat. Amos warned Israel not to trust this restoration—a deeper restoration of the spiritual life of the nation was needed. He declared that a nation would rise up which would push Israel back 'from Lebo Hamath to the valley of the Arabah' (Amos 6:14). These are precisely the limits of the restored boundaries referred to in 2 King 14:25. So there was perhaps conflict between the more pragmatic Jonah and the more spiritual Amos. Within that conflict is a question of identity: what does it mean to be the nation of Israel? It is about territory, land, the freedom and safety to live as the people of God within boundaries. But it is of course deeper than that. It is about relationship, covenant and the landscape of the spirit and the soul. Land and territory, safety and security, were fruits and blessings of the covenant, expressions of it. When boundaries, with their politics and military defence, became fundamental definitions and symbols of the identity of Israel it was clear that God's people had lost sight of their interior spiritual life.

Jonah, interrogated by the sailors on a ship breaking up under the strain of huge forces all around, may well serve as a metaphor for God's judgement on Israel. Israel has failed to be obedient to its true identity. It has concerned itself with the outward appearance of being the covenant people of God while internally it has been wasting away.

So in this context Jonah's response is significant. He declares, 'I am a

Hebrew and I worship the Lord, the God of heaven, who made the sea and the dry land' (Jonah 1:9). 'I am a Hebrew' is a unique phrase in the whole Bible. It may be a phrase to better describe who he is to either the sailors or the original readers of the book. But coupled with his extraordinary declaration of faith towards 'the Lord, the God of heaven, who made both the sea and the dry land' (the last word a pointed statement of faith in the circumstances!), this is surely Jonah beginning to wake up to himself, his true self, for the first time. However, Jonah's words may have had his original audience laughing with derision. They know about this 'son of faithfulness'! They know what his faith has been in—and they're not convinced it's the Lord! Certainly Jonah knows his doctrine and his liturgy—he can make a convincing confession and he knows how to pray (see his prayer in Jonah chapter 2). But I see in this declaration in the heart of the storm the first move back, the first move upwards, an intent to start to discover his true self, who is defined by more than boundaries and career success, more than achievement and status. He is making a tentative but sincere move towards relationship, covenant, with this God of heaven. In doing so, he accepts his fate, his trajectory downwards into the sea, beyond any form or container that he has ever put his trust in. He places his trust in chaos and mystery and the 'God of the *sea* and the land'. His life, as he faces death, may well be just beginning.

Learning to fall

Chaos, an inner, deep chaos, had been beginning to rise in me for some time as I pursued my own missionary journey in Poole. But like Jonah, at the time I was oblivious to it, unconscious, asleep to the signs of a gathering storm outside. Then one day I was woken from my own slumber, humbled and cast into the storm.

Each month I try to take a quiet day. It was January and I was eager to get away and find some quiet to pray and reflect as the year began. But, being less organised than I might have been, I was still at home that morning waiting confirmation from a friend that I could use his nearby cottage. Finally, the call came and I rushed out to drive the ten miles or so to a village outside Poole. I had to take a slight detour to get some fuel and then headed back towards the road out of town. I reached the large and busy roundabout at the centre of Poole when I sensed all was not right with my car. I pulled out on to the roundabout. It was about 9.30 am and the centre of Poole was still pretty busy with morning traffic. As I moved out on to the roundabout and straddled both lanes my car died—suddenly, convincingly and dramatically. Panic hit me, cars swerved to avoid me. Drivers and pedestrians saw me causing havoc in the centre of the roundabout, passing by with withering looks of derision. Compassion and assistance were in pretty short supply that morning. Everyone had somewhere to go to in a hurry and all I was doing was getting in the way. As I sat in the middle of it all, two thoughts occurred to me immediately. Firstly, 'What kind of car decides to break down in the middle of a roundabout when there was a perfectly respectable lay-by only 20 metres further on?' Secondly, 'I know exactly what has happened and whose fault it is… I have just filled my diesel car with a tankful of unleaded petrol!'

For the next three hours, having managed to push my car to the edge of the roundabout and opposite the main entrance to Poole's shopping centre, I sat, hazard warning lights flashing, declaring to the world as it passed by that I was a first-class fool. Traffic hurtled past, sometimes backing up, waiting to move round me. Shoppers looked at me with an air of judgement as I sat there, hour after hour, waiting for rescue. Only a fool fills their otherwise perfectly functioning car with the wrong fuel. Only an idiot makes that kind of simple mistake. Poole cast its verdict on me that day. I suffered a self-imposed, humiliating trial, in the glare of public opinion. I felt naked, exposed, as though all those who looked on me knew my inner failings, my fundamental flaws as a human being.

Everyone makes mistakes. In the grand scheme of things this was not a big deal. Except that the incident pricked at my growing sense that my confidence and competence as a minister was being threatened by a rising storm inside me. Sitting there, helpless and foolish, unable to do anything but wait for rescue, was that moment where the disjunction between what I was doing and who I was began to come into sharp focus. A quote I found at the time summed it up perfectly: 'Your inscape does not match your landscape.'[25] Sitting helpless at the heart of the community I was seeking to reach, I became deeply aware of the truth of that for me.

By early afternoon, a saviour driving an RAC van had sorted me out, charged me a substantial fee, and got me back on the road. There was little of the day left. It was a 30-minute drive to the cottage that was still available to me. Everything in me wanted to head home and bring the whole episode to an end. However, I sensed God speaking, encouraging me to keep going, saying that what he wanted to say could be said in a moment. I drove on, reached the cottage, made a cup of tea and sat down in the silence of the cottage.

Almost immediately I sensed I was hearing the voice of God. It became immediately clear that all that had happened this morning, while a direct result of my own foolish mistake, was nevertheless a precise picture of my own inner life. The whole incident in the morning was a metaphor for the way in which I had been conducting my ministry. I had been constantly filling my own tank up with the wrong kind of fuel for too long and it was killing me. I had been fuelling ministry, driving my activity, by an ambition to see great things happen, pushing myself to succeed with the oxygen of endeavour. On the face of it things looked fine. I was sincere in my faith. I took time out to pray and reflect, to listen to God. But fundamentally, all this activity, everything in my diary, the sum of my daily thought and action, was oriented around a principle of achievement through enterprise and hard work.

Two things had been pointed out to me by the RAC man. Firstly, that diesel and petrol look very much the same. Secondly, you can drive for as much as 100 miles with a mixture of those fuels until the engine finally gives in. In appearance I thought I was going along quite nicely. But all the while there was a deadly toxin of self-motivation and ambition that needed identifying and removing. Hurry is a good indicator of the presence of this poison. I was reminded of the advice of one spiritual adviser to a well-known Christian leader: 'You must ruthlessly eliminate hurry from your life.'[26] I had been in a hurry for a long time: a hurry to see things established, a hurry to see things grow, a hurry to establish my reputation. I had been running for so long, but in which direction? All the time I thought I was making fast and furious progress towards Nineveh, I had been heading for Tarshish and not realised.

Falling upwards

I look back on that incident with huge gratitude now. It was a moment of conversion. It was a moment of revelation and profound redemption for me, because to move ahead in the journey of our vocation will intrinsically involve moments such as these. They are moments, times, perhaps even years of confusion, humiliation, exposure and pain; but they are a gift from the hands of God to break us, shape us and move us on towards our goal. A goal not just of achieving what we feel called to achieve, but being all that God longs for us to be.

These moments work by forcing us to look where we do not want to look. They loosen our grip on the controls of our lives and gently ask the question: 'Are we really in control at all?' They are God's way of encouraging us to face reality, the reality of ourselves and the deeper reality of the universe and who is in control of it.

The medieval mystic Julian of Norwich said, 'First there is the fall, then we recover from the fall. Both are the mercy of God!'[27] Falling really is a mercy, though at the time it feels like anything but. We are used to recognising the recovery as a mercy—forgiveness, redemption and salvation are well-covered themes in the mercy of God. But falling itself? We have been taught to think of this as an aberration, a mistake, and that God's plan of action is essentially one of stopping us from falling, or redeeming us from our mistakes. The deeper mystery, however, is that both fall and recovery are mercies of God. The fall and falling are not worthless and negative, dark episodes in need of a magic formula to defuse them and forget them. Falling is a key element in the grace-filled way of God in enabling us to rise. God brings the very origin of our predicament into the solution. To be free we must face our failings and our fragility. To rise we must fall.

Having said that, none of us are very good at falling. Most of us resist falling with all the energy and guile we can muster. W.H. Auden said, 'We would rather be ruined than changed. We would rather die in our dread than climb the cross of the present and let our illusions die.'[28] Falling involves pain and grief. There may well be physical pain involved in falling. But there will almost certainly be emotional pain, spiritual pain. And there will be grief and loss, for to fall is to lose something precious to us, a status, an identity, a sense of safety and control that perhaps we had worked hard to establish. We will not give it up without a fight.

Furthermore, in our culture we have begun to lose any sense of the need to fall in the first place. The traditional view in Western culture, influenced by the Church and key figures such as Augustine, is that we are created as good but flawed individuals. To grow and to thrive is partly to confront our limitations and our failings, to struggle with ourselves. More recently, however, heavily influenced by the Romantic movement, which emphasised our inner goodness over our inner failings, we have begun to see ourselves as people who simply need to be loved into being the people we are. We talk about the power of positive thinking, go on self-esteem courses and reach inside ourselves to find who we truly are. We are told that when we truly start to love and believe in ourselves then the sky is the limit; there is nothing we cannot achieve if we just put our mind to it and dream big. Within an advanced capitalist and meritocratic society this also has the effect of turning the self into a resource to be used. The self is a mine of great potential. If it can be tapped effectively and marketed efficiently there is no telling what we can achieve. *New York Times* columnist David Brooks said:

> If moral realists saw the self as a wilderness to be tamed, and
> if people in the New Age 1970s saw the self as an Eden to be

actualised, people living in the high-pressure meritocracy are more likely to see the self as a resource base to be cultivated.[29]

How we see ourselves is crucial. Yet we live in a world where that vision of the self as created, good, but flawed—'the "crooked-timber" school of humanity'[30]—has become an unpopular and marginalised vision. So a vision for personal and spiritual growth that involves embracing failure, pain and humiliation is distinctly countercultural.

As Christians, therefore, we need to teach ourselves to see with the eyes of the Spirit, with the eyes of God, who 'draws straight with crooked lines'. We will not readily choose to fall. We may well find ourselves resisting failure and falling as much as anyone else. But with time and practice we begin to embrace the truth that 'the way up is the way down'. We begin to stop in moments of pain and humiliation and arouse all our senses to be alert to what God is doing and saying, so that we can embrace it and listen to it. We begin to learn to stay in the moment of pain, the period of humiliation and lean into it almost, resisting the urge to push it down by any of the modern means of distraction open to us.

That is why Jonah emerging from his slumber in the dark of the ship's hold is significant in so many ways. All his senses are aroused again and he is brought into the light of the deck of the ship. He is asked to listen again and to see anew. And this time that word 'arise' elicits a confession, which, though mere words, has the sense of being forged out of the storm, out of the darkness, out of a place of humiliation. Jonah has fallen. But, while there is further to go down, the journey upwards has begun.

4

Entering the darkness

In most parts of the world, unlike us, people know that a day starts at nightfall. Before there can be any sunrise you must pass through the dark. Before you can be anything you must become nothing.

JOHN V. TAYLOR[31]

Now the Lord provided a huge fish to swallow Jonah, and Jonah was in the belly of the fish three days and three nights.

JONAH 1:17

So, at last, we come to the book of Jonah's most famous moment and its most popular character, the whale. Jonah owes much of his popularity to this one episode, which has inspired art, literature and debate for centuries. That he was swallowed, according to the Hebrew, by a 'huge fish' and not necessarily a whale has not dissuaded anyone, not least the illustrators of children's Bibles, from making the very most of the potential offered by this extraordinary twist in the tale. The drawback of all this attention on the task of imagining Jonah in the belly of a huge fish is that it has made comic and slightly frivolous what is the darkest moment of the story. Perhaps this is not surprising though. We want to skip the darkness and hard graft of Jonah's poetic prayer and hurry on to another schoolboy image, Jonah lying in a pool of whale vomit (snigger!) (Jonah 2:10), and then crack on with the story.

There may be some justification for sidelining Jonah's psalm. Since the text would be just as complete without it, it has been argued that the psalm was added at a later date. That may be, and it is not my task to argue one way or the other. What is interesting for the purposes of exploring vocation and spirituality in this great story is our tendency, in the actual reading of the story, to hurry on in our hope of resolution. The author invites us to pause at length and examine with Jonah something of the emotion of his predicament at the most painful part of his journey. Meanwhile we find ourselves hardly having graduated from the cartoon-condensed versions of the Bible in our minds and anxious to find out what happens next.

But surely this is precisely the point. It is here at the dark heart of the story that we are invited to sit with Jonah and, in contrast to the rest of the book, listen to the heart and soul of Jonah poured out in resplendent poetry. It is precisely these episodes in our own lives and experience that we are habitually hopeless at living with: the dark, difficult, doubting, painful and problematic bits. Part of the purpose of the poetry of chapter 2 is to stall us and urge us to listen and reflect, but in a very different way. The momentum of the story can wait. Nineveh can wait. The story's resolution can wait. All our own agendas, dreams, targets, aims and objectives can wait. When we wait with Jonah in the belly of the whale we are doing something vital, something that in our hurried, activist and utilitarian culture is a deeply countercultural act. We are embracing darkness. We are giving darkness time and space to tell its truths and do its work. We are putting our driven selves on hold for a moment and allowing our doubtful, insufficient selves to catch up with us long enough to teach us. This is a work of God—after all, it is very clear that it is God who provides, or appoints, this huge fish. Yet it is our opportunity to see this dark time for what it is and resist the many temptations to bypass or shortcut, hurrying on as ever to tasks and timetables, prose and purpose.

The work of spiritual formation

When I trained for ordination, a weekly aspect of our training was something we called 'MFG'—ministerial formation groups. These groups were an opportunity for reflection on our personal and spiritual life in a way that began to look ahead to future challenges. Much of this was done with reference to certain forms of spiritual practice: Bible reading, prayer and spiritual direction, for example. MFG were appreciated but not particularly loved by many of us, including myself. When there was a choice between an essay deadline and a task set for the MFG, the essay invariably won. The essay had a much clearer outcome; it was marked and counted towards a final result. The MFG task entered a more ambiguous realm of cause and effect. It also required more than just intellect—it required honesty and a vulnerability towards ourselves.

But in the task of MFG, and the reflections on spirituality and ministry that it asked of us, we were laying the ground for the continued work of spiritual formation. We were being gently reminded that spiritual formation was a work that did not take place simply by itself. The very inclusion in a busy timetable of such a group, week by week, reminded us that unless some kind of accountable format for spiritual growth is attended to, the task of ministry becomes irrelevant.

When we agree to a regular form of action, whether in the spiritual life (for example daily prayer or regular worship) or physical life (a training regime), we are committing ourselves to a form of limitation. There are a great many things we could be doing in those moments when we are praying, or working out, a great many things we would *rather* be doing. But we have chosen this path and we know that unless we commit to it for a sustained period the benefits we expect to get from it will not be forthcoming. In the spiritual life these forms are designed to root our active lives in God. They provide a foundation upon which daily routines, family life and the challenges of work can be grounded and given vitality and perspective.

What we were also doing in those MFG was anticipating that the challenges of a new form, a new container, in our lives—that of ordained ministry—might require a reassessment of the extent to which our current spiritual practices were able to sustain us in the future. If we had never had a spiritual director before, we were encouraged to consider having one. If we had never taken an annual retreat, this was also recommended. A new context suggested there might be a call for new forms. New practices for a new dispensation.

Jonah's psalm does not at first glance seem to flow from anything other than his immediate situation. The specifics of his descent into the stomach of the whale are all there: the deep, the seas, the currents, waves and breakers, engulfing waters, seaweed. More poetically, the confines of the great fish's insides are described as 'deep in the realm of the dead' and the world beneath the waves as 'the roots of the mountains'. Yet as we read this psalm we feel there are parts we have read before, parts that feel like echoes from another place. There is an uncanny familiarity about the language. Words and phrases used to describe Jonah's unique experience and to voice his unique prayer seem drawn from some common well of vocabulary we have also had access to.

This source is, of course, the psalms. Almost every verse contains vocabulary duplicated from the psalter. Many verses are virtual word-for-word transcripts. Jonah's prayer is a brilliant mash-up of well-worn phrases from the prayer and worship book of Israel. But before we cry plagiarism, or before we ask why Jonah could not pray with a bit more spontaneity, a bit more soul, a bit more authenticity, we must remember the vital importance of forms.

Jonah prays with the vocabulary of the psalms because he is steeped in them. These prayers and songs of worship have been the diet of his spiritual life. They have entered his mind and his heart, his very bloodstream, to the extent that they form the basis for the way in which, even under duress, he connects with his God. The psalms have formed his spirituality, his prayer life. We should not be critical of the way this crisis prayer forms on the lips of Jonah; it is precisely the work of liturgical forms to embed the truths of God's nature and a way of articulating them deep into our hearts and minds. In this way forms train us, much in the same way that repeated action trains the fingers of the pianist, or the accuracy of the rugby goal kicker. Dedication to and perseverance with these forms result in spiritual reflexes under pressure. These reflexes can be the fruit of a long-term commitment to the liturgical forms. In the darkness and hopelessness of Jonah's situation, when panic is the reaction you might expect, Jonah is able to draw on a deep reservoir of prayerfulness, connected with the faithfulness of God over generations.

Losing the form book

A closer look at Jonah's psalm, however, begins to reveal that something new is happening. Studies of the form of the psalms themselves have enabled us to identify categories of psalms. The psalms can be divided into two essential forms: praise and lament.[32] Thus, written into Israel's corporate worship were forms that gave vocabulary, metre and structure to the spectrum of circumstance and emotion common to life. The fact that lament—the outpouring of pain, anger and complaint to God—is as prevalent in the psalms as praise comes as something of a shock to many in the modern Western Church. But there it is. Israel did not hide darkness and difficulty from public worship but made as much provision for it as it did for the brightness of praise and thanksgiving. Nothing is left at the door of the temple, or omitted from the content of personal prayer. Life in all its wonder and woe, and God in all his majesty and mystery, are celebrated in the psalms.

This categorisation can be taken a step further to distinguish three forms: psalms of orientation, psalms of disorientation and psalms of reorientation. Where life for the people of God was settled, reliable and prosperous, psalms of orientation expressed gratefulness to God. Where life was confusing, painful, vulnerable and anxious, psalms of disorientation voiced the raw emotion but also the faithfulness of God's people. But where life seemed to come into a new season of peace, a new phase which brought healing or resolution out of a time of hurt and confusion, psalms of reorientation became part of the testimony of the psalter.[33] This last category, a developed aspect of the category of praise, is characterised by expressions of wonder, surprise and awe at the unexpected establishment of a new state of well-being. It is not a return to an old comfort, or familiar sense of coherence, but rather the discovery of a new kind of peace, often just when all sense of this possibility had been lost.

So, here's the punchline. The psalm of Jonah, from the belly of the whale—when he has reached the absolute rock bottom of his journey, when he is as far from God and from his old comforts as he could possibly imagine, when he is a picture of rejection, alienation and failure—is a psalm of *reorientation*. We might have expected a psalm of lament, of disorientation, but instead we get a psalm that falls into the tradition of psalms written when God has miraculously broken in to bring new hope and new life into a situation.

In his psalm, Jonah describes his descent into the belly of the huge fish, concluding his account by saying, the 'earth beneath barred me in forever' (Jonah 2:6b). This is the end of his great descent that began the moment he left for Joppa. Now God breaks in: 'But you, Lord my God, brought my life up from the pit' (2:6c). This is the turning point, the moment of surprising intervention, the axis around which the story tilts, God's intervention at the point at which Jonah has come to the end of his own resources and given up hope (or perhaps even the desire) of ever returning to the old dispensation.

Once again the form of the psalm points us to this conclusion. For verse 6 is the hinge point in the psalm when it is laid out in the classic symmetrical form. This verse tells us about the theme and focus of this psalm more than any other. All previous verses point towards it and all the subsequent verses result from it. Furthermore, it is at this climactic moment that Jonah's psalm breaks form and goes beyond the inherited language and vocabulary I've described:

> The deep surrounded me;
> seaweed was wrapped around my head.
> To the roots of the mountains I sank down;
> the earth beneath barred me in forever.
> JONAH 2:5B–6B

These lines are pure, 100 per cent Jonah! They come directly before the great declaration of God's intervention (v. 6c), which is a quotation from another great psalm of praise (Psalm 103). Just at the point where Jonah's psalm tells us that a new orientation has been reached, Jonah discovers his own voice. The forms of his life up to that point have served him well; they have enabled him to pray, even in the most hopeless of situations. But as God brings new, unexpected, miraculous life, by his grace, Jonah finds himself able to discover his own language and vocabulary for this new experience.

The gift of darkness

The forms of spiritual discipline that support us and train us, root us in God for the present and sustain us into the future, are a voluntary limitation. They are a deliberate curtailing of our natural wants and desires, a calculated freedom *from* certain activities in order to train our freedom *for* God and his ways. Spiritual disciplines are never easy, in the same way that any kind of training is never easy. Our strong will to resort to doing something easier, faster, more comforting, more relaxing is deliberately overcome in order to commit to a higher ideal. Spiritual disciplines are 'voluntary disaster'.[34] For in a small way it feels like disaster. For the ego, that selfish, driven, assertive nature inside each of us, it is most definitely disaster, a moral defeat in a battle to keep control of us.

The reflections we were timetabled to engage in as we prepared for ordained ministry were a means of asking the question, 'Which forms of "voluntary disaster" will you commit to to sustain you in this next challenge?' 'How will you structure your more hidden spiritual disciplines so that your visible activity can be fruitful and sustainable?'

Yet there are transitions in the Christian life and in the journey of our vocation which take us beyond 'voluntary disaster'. There are transformations that God would have us make that by their very nature need somehow to short-circuit the will and the intellect in order to be successful. They require circumstances and limitations that are involuntary so that, out of his gracious love for us, God can bring about painful and disorientating change in ways that we would otherwise avoid. And one of the key circumstances, or limitations, that God uses to do this within is that of darkness.

The story is very clear that 'the Lord provided a huge fish' (Jonah 1:17). There is no denying from Jonah's description what a horrific and traumatic experience it was for Jonah to be engulfed by this provision. Yet, as we have seen, something new and extraordinary takes place within Jonah in the belly of the huge fish. A new voice, a liberation from old forms, a new commitment (2:9), perhaps, even a new perspective. All this takes place within the confined space of the belly of a whale! Debates about whether such a whale really existed and whether any human being, let alone Jonah, could really survive three days in the stomach of one, and not only survive but pick himself up and carry on apparently unharmed, are irrelevant to the meaning of the story. What is central to the story, a story designed to teach us, is that the work God needed to do in Jonah (and so in us) *can only* take place in these sorts of places: dark, isolated, disorientating, hopeless, restricted and beyond the reach of our intellect or activity. These are places we would never choose ourselves. Even if we felt God was leading us there, we would most likely not step in that direction. No, we must, as it were, be blindfolded and led. Psychiatrist and author Gerald May said: 'To guide us toward the love that we most desire, we must be taken where we could not and would not go on our own.'[35]

Darkness is the word that best describes the form of limitation we are exploring. But it is not simple darkness in the sense in which we often use the word, as a time of great pain, or loss or trauma, something essentially negative and even evil. It could be every one of those things, but the deeper understanding of God's darkness, the 'dark night of the soul' as it is often called, is something more subtle than that. The word used by two of the greatest writers on this subject, St John of the Cross and St Teresa of Avila, writing in their native Spanish, is *oscura*. *Oscura* simply means 'obscure' and highlights the essential experiences of confusion and uncertainty that are the nature of the 'dark night of the soul'. These two writers use a different word, *tinieblas*, when referring to the darkness of evil. The distinctions between the experiences denoted by these words may be hard to identify. The difference lies in the potential ability of *oscura* to address the effects of the kind of darkness that *tinieblas* seeks to describe. Gerald May said:

In *oscuras* things are hidden; in *tinieblas* one is blind. In fact, it is the very blindness of *tinieblas*, our slavery to attachment and delusion, that the dark night of the soul is working to heal.[36]

The darkness of the belly of the whale in the depths of the sea is a darkness used by God to bring about personal transformation in Jonah. This kind of darkness by its very nature, in any place or time or context, can harbour all those experiences of alienation, confusion and uncertainty. Darkness cuts off our dependence on the senses which work collectively under conditions of light to help us navigate the world. As a result, darkness probes at our confidence in the intellect and the mind. Darkness makes us vulnerable, helpless, searching for new dependencies, longing for a way out. No wonder we avoid darkness and demonise it as something essentially negative. We employ various and creative means to dispel darkness from our lives. We use what author and priest Barbara Brown Taylor calls 'artificial lights',[37] the distractions of our shallow age—consumerism, alcohol, drugs, sex and the media—to illuminate us briefly. But all the time there is a tugging sense that all these lights, all these desires, are only substitutes for something more real and more profound.

Even lights that have proved faithful and helpful for us in our spiritual growth become tired and unhelpful. The forms of our own spiritual tradition are there to open us to the source of this fundamental light. But for some of us, even they become an idol rather than an icon, something that blinds or blocks the light rather than enables us to really see. What seems to be characteristic of the sort of darkness we are exploring, the darkness used by God, is that old forms no longer seem sufficient to accommodate the new thing that is being birthed in the darkness. We are invited to explore beyond the limitations of what has sustained us to this point, to let go and free ourselves to receive what God would give us in the darkness. And it is only the blindside confusion of darkness that will free us from our own structures and dependencies enough to open us up to the new thing God wants to do.

The storm of my own experience, which I described in the last chapter, was the beginning of a descending darkness into which I travelled. I experienced this deepening darkness in a number of ways. I began to lose conviction in certain forms that had served me and the Church well over many years. Partly, this was due to a sense that they were not 'working', but more profoundly there was a sense in which I felt there was something yet to be discovered. I had put significant trust in certain techniques of Bible study, prayer and mission and these had not met my high ambitions for success. I had also invested heavily in prayer, believing, as I still do, that mission without prayer is simply active endeavour. In particular, my sense that I needed to intercede for what we were doing was turning into a responsibility that lay heavily on me. From time to time I would find a new conviction or a new source of inspiration and commit myself anew to patterns and lists to ensure that nothing went 'unprayed' for. But gradually I was sinking under the weight of an impossible task and an unrealistic spiritual theology. The enterprise illusion, which suggests the more we work, the more we plan and scheme and employ clever programmes, the more we will see God at work, had entered my personal spirituality. But did a God of grace really need me to pray harder and harder to enable his will to be done? Was this ministry to which I felt called dependent on my prayerful activity and that of those under my leadership? Was I really that indispensable?

I am still working through this transformation even now but I know that things have begun to change. I reached a place of darkness and claustrophobia in prayer that brought about a willingness to be open to whatever God would lead me into. I began to discover the prayer of silence and contemplation, the prayer of the heart, and I sensed a freedom to pursue this as the foundation for my own spirituality. I could say much more about this and the effects it is having in me and the communities I lead, but that is for later. For now the key point is the role of darkness, a bewildering experience of confusion and uncertainty that took me to a place that my own will or intellect could not have taken me. Indeed, some of the literature I found myself reading over this time was literature I had read before and, ironically, found completely obscure. For me it was the work of God in the darkness of this time that suddenly brought this same writing into a new light and offered me illumination when I needed it.

Darkness and ministry

For leaders in ministry it is hardly any wonder that we find ourselves avoiding darkness when it often feels as if we are required to be light for everyone else. I am increasingly convinced that Jonah was a leading light in the corridors of power at the time of Jeroboam II. His descent is a salutary tale for those wrestling with the dilemmas of professional ministry, where personal spirituality and public responsibility become uncomfortably connected. How do we lead worship, inspire others and act as a model for others when we sense a gathering darkness in our own spiritual lives? How much of the vicar or pastor's authenticity and vulnerability can a community cope with before they start looking for someone a bit more reliable, a little more 'positive'?

It is all too easy for ministers in a position of leadership to collude with communities and congregations in the art of darkness avoidance. The loss of the psalms of lament from public worship may have much to do with this. It is as though we have forgotten how to speak the language of darkness and vulnerability and evolved structures that ensure we don't relearn how to do this.[38]

Furthermore, the experience of public ministry can so easily dull our senses to the growing darkness inside us. Leadership and ministry are fertile ground for the ego. The noble call to humble service with which we may have entered ministry is challenged on a regular basis by the sweet experience of being someone, doing good and being needed. Our institutions and traditions bring us, unwittingly sometimes, into contexts that confer status, even if in a relatively small universe. They also project expectation, generally unrealistic, on lead individuals. These expectations can cripple. But not before they have inflated our ego, which whispers that perhaps, truly, it is 'for this moment that I came'. As Rowan Williams says in reflecting on the wisdom of the desert monasteries for modern-day ministry: 'Monastic witness is not going to be easily compatible with a life in which it is easy to be ensnared in the fantasies of others and caught up in an illusory position of dignity.'[39]

Perhaps most insidious of all in diminishing our awareness of the state of our own inner life is the cult of busyness. Busyness has been exalted to the point of being fashionable in our own culture. We are nobody unless we are simply too busy even to say how we are. There is a relentlessness and a busyness to the story of Jonah which is intoxicating and entertaining. A vast adventure is packed into just 48 verses. It is the Minor Prophets on Twitter. That is, except for those eight verses of poetry at the very heart of the book which bring about a deliberate and profound pause. As we noted, the central axis of this poetical reflection contains the key moment of revelation within it. But more than that, this same verse is the very centre of the whole narrative. Jonah 2:6c is almost the very middle of the book, being the end of verse 23 of the 48-verse book. The moment when Jonah declares, 'But you, Lord my God, brought my life up from the pit,' is the moment when the story turns and heads in a different direction. Descent has turned to ascent, death into resurrection. And it took poetry to do it! Patient, reflective metaphor instead of hurried prose. The lesson is clear. Only when we slow down, only when we rest from all our self-important busyness, only when we cease from our driven agendas, can we cultivate an awareness that makes possible the transforming work of God.

Busyness was certainly one of the factors blinding me to my journey into darkness. Busyness was also a convenient way of ignoring the sense that all was not well within me. As long as I kept busy I could feel justified both to myself and to others. On the other hand, as I reflect on my experience of pioneer ministry over the past seven years, I realise that a great deal of its very nature has the ingredients of 'dark night'. The nature of pioneering is to venture into the unknown, to go off the map, to leave old structures and forms behind. We are choosing a road that leads to disorientation, confusion and uncertainty. Mature pioneers will resist the temptation to hastily employ generic forms, structures and programmes that have been successful elsewhere. What is required is a willingness to listen deeply and trust that the right forms will emerge in this new context.

The 20th-century Catholic missionary Vincent Donovan told the remarkable story of his pioneering work among the Maasai people of Tanzania. With extraordinary courage he chose to ignore the traditional methods and forms of mission of the time. With incredible faith and determination he went beyond the safety and control of the mission compound, where health and educational establishments were used to try to bring the gospel to nomadic tribespeople. He recognised that the very nature of mission was 'a process leading to that new place where none of us has ever gone before'.[40] As he began his work, he summarised his approach to his bishop in a letter announcing his intentions: 'I have no theory, no plan, no strategy, no gimmick—no idea of what will come. I feel rather naked. I will begin as soon as possible.'[41]

Naked vulnerability, not knowing where you are going, being without strategy or plan, these are the realities of pioneer ministry. It is an *oscura* experience, a deep experience of obscurity and dark night, that is intrinsic to the call of the pioneer minister. And commitment to that 'not knowing', to that waiting in the darkness for God, is the discipline that enables God to do a new thing, both in the midst of those we are ministering to, and also in us. Once again our vocation is not simply about what can happen by God's grace out there among a people or a community. It is just as importantly about what can happen in us, the transformation that takes place through our wrestling in the darkness.

Of course, this is not purely the experience of pioneer ministry. It is the reality of mission. One of the rediscoveries that has been so important to the pioneering mission movement of recent years is the theological concept of the *missio Dei*—that God by his very nature is a missionary God. He is always on the move, always venturing on, always leading his people with him, into new places, new challenges and new revelations of who he is. That 'the Church exists by mission as fire exists by burning'[42] is not a pragmatic reality, but a theological one. For to be the

Church is to journey with God as the people of God, to be a community that follows Jesus, follows the Spirit that he sent. Since the nature of the Trinity is missional then we are simply not the Church if we are not missional. And it is in the very nature of mission to constantly take us as a missionary Church beyond our traditional practices, our methods and our strategies and into the realm of the unknown, where the Spirit of God is doing a new thing.

I believe very firmly that God is doing a new thing in the Church of the Western world. The missional movement that I am a small part of did not come about by committee or Synodic decree. It came about by individuals responding to a call of God to venture out, in many cases free from the trappings of assumed missional methods, and follow the Spirit into communities disconnected from the Church. I believe this is a sign of the new thing God is doing in a Church that is collectively experiencing something of a dark night of the soul. A Church that is struggling to live in a culture where old forms no longer hold the power they once did. A Church that is increasingly uncertain of its voice and disorientated in a culture that it is no longer central too. A Church that is working hard to carry out its traditional ministries better and smarter, while at the same time privately asking itself whether they are really fit for purpose. A Church that looks at the future and might well admit that it doesn't know how it can sustain its existence. It does indeed feel like darkness. But as those who have journeyed with darkness and explored its mysteries tell us, darkness is the necessary means of changing us where we would not otherwise be willing to change.

Learning to embrace the darkness

Personally and collectively, then, we must learn to embrace darkness. We will always fear it, but we do not need to avoid it. Gradually we can learn to lean into it, to wrestle with it, unwilling to let it go until it has bestowed on us its surprising blessing, like Jacob wrestling with God in Genesis 32:22–31. We need to be willing to recognise that as much as God is a God of light, God also dwells in darkness. On Mount Sinai, at the establishment of the covenant of the law, God comes to Moses 'in a dense cloud' (Exodus 19:9). The Hebrew word to describe this darkness is *araphel*, a word unique to the description of the kind of darkness in which God chooses to reveal himself, while at the same time remaining hidden. On the mount of transfiguration Jesus becomes transfigured by an overwhelming light, before all those present are enveloped by 'a bright cloud' from which they hear the voice of God reiterating the truth of the identity of Jesus as the Son of God (Matthew 17:5). It is not darkness or light so much as obscurity and fear that epitomise these experiences of acute revelation.

Fundamentally these are experiences of vulnerability, experiences which are a gift to us to prise us out of our fortresses of comfort and control. Recently, research has begun to explore why some people seem more resilient to failure, shame and humiliation. These people seem to have a deeper capacity for self-belief, a foundational sense that they are 'enough' and that nothing they do or do not do will shake that. These 'wholehearted' people share a number of fundamental ideals, but perhaps the most significant of these is a high value for vulnerability. Author Brené Brown has said:

> The Wholehearted identify vulnerability as the catalyst for courage, compassion and connection... They attribute everything—from their professional success to their marriages to their proudest parenting moments—to their ability to be vulnerable.[43]

Embracing darkness means embracing vulnerability. Each time we resist the temptation to suppress feelings of vulnerability we are taking a step of courage to be open to how that vulnerability, in the hands of God, might be shaped to teach us and how it may be shaped to change us. Moments like that occur every day. However, sometimes periods of this experience of vulnerability and disorientation seem to consume us. These times of darkness, uncertainty and confusion, where the old maps no longer make sense and it feels as if all we can do is sit and wait in the gloom, still have their hope within them. They are involuntary crises stewarded by God to bring the change we could never have wrought by ourselves.

I am slowly learning to let the darkness come, to lean into it, wrestle with and trust it for the gift I firmly believe it to be. It is never comfortable and I do not think it will ever really become so. The dark night is not something we go through once and then think, 'Good! Now that's over with I can get on and enjoy my life.' The dark night is a continual process of transformation, of varying intensity, throughout our lives. Much of the time when we thought life was easy we were simply not open to or aware of the darkness knocking at our door. Now we are finding it harder to escape from. So we must learn to embrace it, value it and discover the gift within it.

5
Knowing your limits

Go. Sit in your cell and give your body in pledge to the walls.
Advice of an Elder to a Younger Monk[44]

Then the word of the Lord came to Jonah a second time: 'Go to the great city of Nineveh and proclaim to it the message I give you.'

Jonah obeyed the word of the Lord and went to Nineveh. Now Nineveh was a very large city; it took three days to go through it. Jonah began by going a day's journey into the city, proclaiming, 'Forty more days and Nineveh will be overthrown.' The Ninevites believed God. A fast was proclaimed, and all of them, from the greatest to the least, put on sackcloth.
JONAH 3:1–5

Jonah appears to be back on track. He has reached Nineveh. All goes well. He preaches, the king repents and calls on his people to do the same and to pray to God for forgiveness. Before you know it, God has changed his mind and relented from his threatened destruction of Nineveh. That might have been the end of the story—the story of a recalcitrant prophet who gets it wrong, turns around and then gets it right. This would make the story of Jonah a simple story of obedience, showing that when we trust God, go where he calls us, speak the words he gives us, remarkable things happen.

But this is a more complex and mysterious story than that. Just as we begin to believe that Jonah is a reformed character it becomes evident that he isn't. For Jonah's response to the gracious work of God is one of anger. 'To Jonah this seemed very wrong, and he became angry' (Jonah 4:1). If chapters 1 and 2 are about how Jonah sees himself and his relationship with God, then chapters 3 and 4 are about how Jonah sees himself in relationship to God *and others*. While the storm and the whale appear to have made Jonah relinquish his grasp on selfish ambition, they do not appear to have made him revise his attitude to the Ninevites. Jonah thought that he and God shared a condemnatory view of the Ninevites and, more significantly, a retributive view of what they deserved. He was wrong. Something he is still struggling to get used to after a long and successful career of being right!

Jonah has plenty of time to reflect on his views about Nineveh and the Ninevites as he travels from the shore across 900 miles of desert to this great city. Yet he arrives with as characteristic a view as when he received a call to go there in the first instance. All places have history, a reputation. Many places become bywords or triggers for our imaginations and our prejudices. A year living in Ruchazie, part of Greater Easterhouse, a massive sprawl of connected tenement estates on the eastern edge of Glasgow, taught me all I needed to know about the reputation of places. I lived there as a church volunteer for a year in the early 1990s, working with the local parish church. The church sat behind fences decorated with razor wire, every door had security roller shutters. My own flat was burgled in my first couple of weeks, and the communal staircase in my tenement block was a regular location for drinking and drug-taking. So, the estate had its problems. Yet it was full of some of the friendliest, kindest and most generous people I've ever met. I joined a local hockey club, based outside Easterhouse, which drew members from across the city. Without a car I was dependent on lifts to get to training or matches. None of the rest of the team had ever driven through Ruchazie. None of them wanted to. It was months before I could persuade anyone to pick me up or drop me at my home, and when someone finally did agree, you could see the look of astonishment on his face when he managed to drive out again unscathed.

Nineveh had a similarly bad reputation. It had one thing in common with Tarshish: few people had ever been there or seen it. But the myth surrounding Nineveh was diametrically opposite to Jonah's earlier view of Tarshish as a safe haven. Jewish writer Hayyim Lewis summed up the view powerfully:

The Assyrians were the Nazi storm-troopers of the ancient world. They were the pitiless-crazed foe. They showed no quarter in

> battle, uprooting entire people in their fury for conquest. They extinguished the Northern Kingdom of Israel... For Jonah, Nineveh, then, was no ordinary city; it carried doom-laden, tragic memories, it stood as a symbol of evil incarnate.[45]

Jonah, then, might be forgiven for having an inherited, entrenched view of Nineveh, one he is still carrying as he emerges from the desert and enters the city. But it is not the same view as God's. And what the writer is concerned to get across to us is that, whatever this place may be, whatever reputation it has, whatever history, it is nevertheless a place that is within the mind and heart of a God who saves. Whatever vision or image of a place we have must be laid down. How we see a place, how we have been influenced to see it, may have little to do with how God sees a place. And the only way we may align our vision with God's is to start again and ask God to help us see a place as he sees it.

Map-making for missionaries

As Jonah enters Nineveh, the narrator emphasises what the book's audience would have expected. This is a truly huge city. It is a 'great city' (Jonah 1:2, 3:2), a rare description in biblical literature. 'It took three days to go through it' (3:3). However, archaeological excavations reveal a city that at its widest dimension was two-and-three-quarter miles across. You could walk it in an hour, never mind three days. The narrator may be exaggerating, or perhaps the understanding of what was meant by 'city' included a much wider area dependent on it for trade and for refuge in times of insecurity. But this is to miss the point. Nineveh is a great city, it is large by the standards of the day, and its reputation is great. Walking into Nineveh would make the hairs on your neck stand up and your heart beat faster. Passing beneath its gates would elicit feelings of awe, respect and fear. It was like Jesus walking into Jerusalem, or Paul walking into Rome.

The time taken to tell us Nineveh's dimensions also suggests simply the importance of noticing the details of a place. Specifying these dimensions tells us of Nineveh's vastness but also its uniqueness. This in turn suggests how we might approach a place, as missionaries, as ministers with a call to a place and a people. In many ways we need to start by doing what the narrator does, and what Jonah does. We need to walk a place's dimensions. We need to look and measure, size a place up, literally and metaphorically. We need to make a map. It may not be a literal map, though it could be. But the discipline of map-making, of taking the time to measure, mark, scale, count and listen, is a key one.

There are, however, different kinds of maps, which can harbour different attitudes to place. The maps we are familiar with are grid maps. Invented in the 16th century, more or less at the same time as the rise of modern science, grid maps provide a means of transferring the confusion of our three-dimensional landscape into a neat and controlled two-dimensional grid. This was a hugely powerful and fruitful invention. But it has its dangers. Grid maps reduce our complex locality into rather bland coordinates. They suck the mystery out of a place, they order chaos by measurement and precision. They tell us we can master a place. Furthermore, they suggest we might therefore exploit a place now we know where everything is and how to get there. They also start to eliminate the element of surprise in a place. As American poet Robert Penn Warren writes, 'Our maps have grown less speculative, less interested in the elemental possibilities of the Earth's skin, and that suggests that the Earth has lost the capacity to keep secrets.'[46]

The authority of grid maps tells us what there is and therefore what to expect; they are maps that tempt us towards utility rather than wonder, mastery rather than mission. However, there are other kinds of maps. Earlier map-making was based on story as well as place. Maps were oral and fused places with occurrence and with people: 'that tree' or 'that mountain', 'the place where such an event occurred', 'that area beyond the river ford where the grass is good for grazing'. When I first arrived in Poole one of the first things I did was visit the local history library. I asked the librarian if she could let me see all the maps of Poole that she had. She returned some time later with a pile of maps which I then arranged in chronological order across a large table. As I did this a story took shape in front of me as Poole grew from a small medieval port to an industrial centre with residential districts spreading northwards and eastwards into the surrounding hills. The Poole of my present was put into context as a place shaped by various forces and dynamics over hundreds of years.

Furthermore, inspired by reading about more narrative maps and to help train myself in the discipline of a more attentive map-making, I began making another map of the wider area with the intention of noticing and deepening my understanding of this place I was in. I began making a map of Poole Harbour in relation to its natural life. As a birdwatcher and forager I began to outline the landscape, none too accurately, and then sketch and write notes on this: 'chanterelles found Oct 2012', 'marsh samphire here', 'roosting site for wintering hen harrier', 'osprey seen here Aug 2011'. The map soon filled up with wonder and with story. The flat coordinated world of my beaten-up OS Landranger map began to be replaced with a map of my own making, replete with my experiences, testimony and surprise.

These latter kinds of map are the kind we must be making as we start to live and minister in a place. Missionary maps must have a limited horizon. They must not get carried away with themselves and start drawing themselves on ambitious scales. Nor must they act like grid maps for a mission programme or off-the-shelf model—a two-dimensional resource map ready for mining. Missionary maps are the cartography of incarnational love. They blend history and place and people to begin to reveal something of the soul of a place. They begin to unveil the secrets of the work of the Spirit over time in a place. They begin to offer to us a door into the hidden kingdom that is already at work, quietly and steadily transforming a place behind the plane of the visible surface. They begin to write us an invitation to enter into that story in that place in such a way that we are servants of it and not masters over it.

It takes time to allow such a map to be made. And the process never ends. Unlike grid maps, story maps are not snapshots in time with their suggestion of completion. Listening, editing and adding continues. This requires a change in us. It takes humility to make a story map, a willingness to sit at the feet of a place and let it tell its tale in the words of history, landscape and personal testimony. It requires sacrifice, an emptying of our own assumptions and expectations. It necessitates a relinquishing of our ambition and its allies—power and control. Making story maps teaches us to be *incarnational* missionaries, earthed pioneers, immersed in a place, listening to it and learning from it. The process teaches us to love a place purely for itself and for the secrets of the kingdom that may be revealed in it if only we stop to look and listen. It teaches us to be open to seeing a place as God sees it.

When we map a place with the scientific methods of the modern grid map we are always in danger of reducing a place to a set of resources to exploit for our own agenda. It is another kind of utilitarian calculus. When we learn to map a place with the eye of loving service, when we walk into a place with humility, with an appropriate fear, with wonder and with our attention directed at sensing a place as God senses it, we begin to truly listen, truly understand and truly love. We must guard against approaching a place as a vessel, empty of what we think we can add to it. We must beware of being so foolish as to think we know what a place needs. Almost inevitably when we do that, we 'discover' that a place needs precisely what we had planned to provide. As the saying goes, 'When all we have is a hammer, everything begins to look like a nail'! This is the great temptation of a church that thinks it has answers: it spends a great deal of time and energy providing answers to questions no one is asking. So to retrain ourselves out of these instinctive behaviours we must learn how to map in a different way, a way that is more about narrative and story, which forces us to listen intently to what people are really saying about a place, which opens up the possibility of hearing God's voice amid the people and place we have been called to reach.

Ordinary heroes

This is humbling work, to work with the limitations of place. Limitation is a gift not a hindrance. When we learn graciously to accept the limitations of the people and place we are called to minister to, we are placing our ministry within the scope of God's call. For God's call is always to a specific place. God's call is always earthed in real people and real space. To work in that way, no matter how frustrating or messy, is an act of faith in the gift of our vocation.

Similarly we must work with *our own* limitations. The image that the narrator creates as Jonah walks into Nineveh is of this great city of gigantic proportions dwarfing the beleaguered Jonah who has himself been cut down to size, both in his own estimation and in that of his readers, by all that has happened up to this moment. One huge, powerful city. One small, feeble human being.

Once again, if the book of Jonah had ended with the conclusion of chapter 3, you could be forgiven for casting Jonah not just as the hero (in the literary sense) but as the 'superhero' of the story. He has faced his challenge, cast off his demons, reconciled himself to God and triumphed in the end. But this is a far more subtle story than that. Leadership in Western culture always has a tendency to exalt the leader as hero/heroine. The heroic leader succeeds where the rest of us mere mortals cannot. He triumphs over the limitations of the crisis situation and over the limitations of himself in order to bring victory, or resolution, on behalf of the people. But the consequence of this vision of the leader is a people unable themselves to fully own the vision or ability that is contained within the unique heroic individual. The result is a deeply unhealthy dynamic where 'leader and led exist in a thoroughly unhealthy co-dependent relationship'.[47] The led can be happy with their limitations and failings while revelling in the transcendent abilities of the hero. There is ample scope for delusion and collusion here.

Chapter 4 pulls the rug from underneath that vision of leadership.

Jonah is a far more complex hero than that. His story invites us to see his leadership as one that does not simply *transcend* limitation in a way that few of us will ever be able to, in a way that casts him as the magical and rare individual. Jonah's story instead invites us to see him wrestling with, facing up to and embracing his limitations. Jonah is a fragile, everyman kind of missionary and minister, battling with his confusion, his anger, his failure and his humanity in the face of an overwhelming challenge and an overwhelming God. He is one of us. An ordinary hero, seeking to work out his vocation within the limits of his humanity.

What the superhero offers in our imagination is a shortcut, a vicarious means of achieving what we long to see. The call on our lives, or the lives of a community, can be marginalised. All hope is focused on the hero. The rest of us become spectators, worshippers, then critics, then judges. In an anxious church, concerned about its own future survival, we are prone to look for superheroes. They fly in, as if from another realm, and, by the sheer force of their supernatural gifts, talent, personality and charisma, solve the unsolvable and perform the miracle that is desired. Or at least we would like them to. Christian superheroes are few and far between. Those that exist usually lead someone else's church.

Pioneers can be just as prone to this as anyone else. They are often called to places where others have failed, or called into areas where the traditional church has failed, retreated, or is not in a place to engage. I would joke that the title 'pioneer minister' had a superhero ring to it, that I needed a Lycra suit with a big P on the front. It was a joke, but with a serious underbelly to it. As I began to confront failure, and my own limitations, as things did not work out as I had hoped, or perhaps expected, I was increasingly aware of the extent to which I had bought into this vision of leader as superhero, as magician. Slowly and painfully my vision was renewed. I began to realise that the greatest miracle of all is that of God choosing to work within the scope of my own limitations and the limitations of the place and people to which I was called. It is a thing of utter wonder to grasp that a part of God's plan for the salvation of the cosmos has been reduced to the fallible responsibility of someone like me, or you, or Jonah.

The 'Grand Miracle'

C.S. Lewis traced the heart of the miraculous back to one central miracle, the miracle of the incarnation:

> The central miracle asserted by Christians is the Incarnation. They say that God became Man. Every other miracle prepares for this, or exhibits this, or results from this. Just as every natural event is the manifestation at a particular place and moment of Nature's total character, so every particular Christian miracle manifests at a particular place and moment the character and significance of the Incarnation. There is no question in Christianity of arbitrary interferences just scattered about. It relates not a series of disconnected raids on Nature but the various steps of a strategically coherent invasion—an invasion which intends complete conquest and 'occupation'.[48]

His thesis was for a theology of the miraculous which was consistent with how we recognise the natural world to be and who we know God to be. God does not intervene in the world as an alien, but as someone out of whom nature springs and whose character we perceive in nature itself. He comes 'not as a foreigner but as a sovereign'[49] such that 'each miracle writes for us in small letters something that God has already written, or will write, in letters almost too large to be noticed, across the whole canvas of Nature'.[50]

And God's key strategy of intervention is not the kind of miracle which the Jews were forever asking Jesus for and which he was always refusing to provide. His key strategy is the painfully slow and humble process of election, of choosing a people, a nation, a place, not for its own sake but in order for it to be a blessing, a source of the life of God to those around it. The zenith of that strategy is Jesus, the Messiah, the chosen one. He comes not as Messianic hero, to take on all the

Messianic visions and expectations that have accumulated since the exile. The miraculous takes on flesh. He comes as a vulnerable, limited human being. He comes and embraces the local and obscure ('Can anything good come out of Nazareth?'). He willingly restricts himself to the human frame, to time and place, hunger and thirst, tiredness and frailty. As C.S. Lewis said, 'The Power that always was behind all healings puts on a face and hands… The world which would not know Him as present everywhere was saved by His becoming local.'[51]

In a global world where everything short of international recognition is seen as something of a disappointment, where we can fly to the other side of the world to hang on the coat-tails of the latest heroic Christian miracle worker, God is asking us to sign up to a strategy of deliberate and consistent local obscurity. We are called to commit ourselves to this place and this time. And we are called to commit ourselves to the wonderful limitations of the person that we are.

There are no shortcuts in this approach and the ones presented to us will always diminish who we are and exploit the place and people we are called to serve. We are called, as Mother Teresa famously said, to do 'small things with great love'. Francis of Assisi once said, 'First do what's necessary, then do what's possible, soon you will be doing what's impossible.' That is an approach to ministry and mission that seems to line up with the incarnation and the divine strategy of election. It does not make God any less powerful or capable of the miraculous. It simply places us in obedience to the paradoxical way in which God has designed his plan of salvation and renewal, which is via the individual, the local and the small.

Pledging ourselves to the walls

Living our vocation is in essence making a covenant with ourselves, God and the place and people to which he has called us. Like a covenant of marriage, this commitment is not primarily based on ability and gifting, a kind of matching of resources that might make it 'work'. It is founded on love and fidelity.

Call, first and foremost, is an expression of love. Love of God. Love of ourselves despite our unloveliness. Love of this people, this place. The love of God himself for this place and this people, which he lovingly invites us to share. When it is reduced simply to matching a CV to a job description it is not worthy of the description 'vocation'.

Rowan Williams relates a story from the desert tradition of a monk struggling to continue with his vocation. He seeks advice from an elder brother, who says, 'Go. Sit in your cell and give your body in pledge to the walls.'[52] That is precisely the holy thing we are doing, the covenant we are making when we respond obediently to the call of God to a place. We are committing ourselves, pledging ourselves, 'to the walls', the limitations of our own self and the limitations of people, geography, history and poverty. To do anything else is to transcend the reality, either of ourselves or the context we are in. And when we do that we venture into the territory that would cast us as heroes and magicians. As Williams states, 'You have to "espouse" reality rather than unreality, the actual limits of where and who you are rather than the world of magic in which anything can happen if I want it to.'[53]

When we first started Reconnect, we wanted to practise incarnational ministry—listening to and loving place. However, what came as a surprise at the time was a clear sense that God was pointing out that to be an incarnational community also meant listening to one another. It meant listening to the reality of who we were as a small missional community. As a result we were drawn away from unrealistic projections of what miracles a small group like us could achieve and gently guided towards the unique and wondrous things God wanted to do that went with the grain of the reality of our community.

One of the particular things about us was that within an initial group of nine adults we had two people, including my wife Emily, who were felt-makers. Felt-making is a beautiful and diverse art form based on working with dyed sheep's wool and using the natural tendency of the wool to meld and weft together when worked with liquid soap. We figured that having felt-makers in our community at a rate of nearly 25 per cent was probably higher than the national average and so needed to be listened to!

As we talked and prayed more the decision was made to offer felt-making workshops to people and see if that might be a way of building relationships with them. Those workshops grew in popularity and regularity. Then Emily sensed that perhaps there was another step to take with this. She approached the owner of a local café and asked if this growing network of people gathering around textile art might meet regularly in a first-floor lounge above the main café. This gathering would be based on creativity, community and offering people a precious space in the midst of life to attend to themselves and, in particular, those areas of themselves that are so easily forgotten—creativity and spirituality. And so Space for Life was born and has continued to grow and thrive ever since. At the heart of Space for Life is a core of Christian women who pray and offer a nurturing, loving, welcoming space. During their gatherings there is a time of silence in which a short section of the Bible is read and people are invited to reflect or pray (or ignore!). Without any encouragement some have called Space for Life 'church'. Most who come would ordinarily find the idea of 'church' a very negative one. More recently the core group at the heart of Space for Life has started a separate discipleship group that meets weekly to read and discuss the Gospels, and around ten people have joined.[54]

Who would have thought that a new community exploring Christian spirituality and discipleship, a community that is making steps towards becoming a mature expression of church for those who come, would emerge from two people inviting others to come and make felt together? It is miraculous. Truly miraculous. It is a miracle that has taken place through the intervention of God within the natural limitations of human beings who have committed themselves to it. It is not heroic, or magical. It is very ordinary. Yet absolutely extraordinary.

Tending the allotment

Working within the limitations of this place in this time, within the limitations of our own shortcomings and of the resources within our community, is a beautiful thing when we pledge ourselves to it. Our commitment may weaken, however, if we give in to frustration, which can lead to contempt: contempt at our own inability, or, more particularly, contempt towards people and place. Frustration begins with 'if only...' statements: 'if only we had more money', 'if only people were more responsive', 'if only we had better musicians', 'if only people were more committed'. It soon turns into 'Why can't...?' questions: 'Why can't people give more?' 'Why can't people understand what we are saying?' 'Why can't people do things better?' Frustration is inevitable but it does not need to lead to contempt. The faithfulness of 'pledging ourselves to the walls' encourages us to lean in and wrestle with these frustrations. They are an inevitable part of working within the reality of the material world. They are also a basic ingredient of the material for our growth as Christians and as leaders.

When I was first ordained we moved as a family into a new area and decided to put our name down with the local authority for an allotment. We did some research of local allotment sites and noticed that the nearest one seemed to have plenty of plots that looked untended. So we badgered the Council's allotment officer, who did an inspection and then to our delight offered us a half plot. The plot was about the closest to our house that was possible. We accepted it immediately. It felt like such a gift. So on my days off I began work on this plot. Nobody had tended it for some time. It was completely overgrown, a mass of brambles and couch grass. Undeterred, I decided to dig out beds gradually. On the very first occasion that I sank a fork into the ground I hit a wasps' nest and was chased across the plot by a small platoon of aggressive wasps. I then discovered that every single square inch of the plot was about half a foot deep in gravel. In conversation with one or two other plot holders I was told that the area had until recently been a car park for that end of the allotments. Brilliant! I was cultivating a car park! The Council had generously seen fit to give me possibly the most difficult, unwanted section of ground in the city!

It was this or the bottom of the waiting list, though. So I bought a wheelbarrow and started carting load after load of stones to the stream at the bottom of the allotments. It was unbelievably hard work. Up and down a steep hill for day after day, watched by all those lovely allotment holders with plots that had things like soil and plants growing in them! I coveted their beautifully tended plots. Then I hated them. Then I hated my own plot for being about as fit for growing anything as the Arctic tundra! Then I began to develop a sharp contempt for the whole project, the Council, allotments, allotment holders, vegetables, soil… everything! It was all futile!

But this was our allotment. It was the limited area of ground that we had been given. We could give up. We could go in search of a different allotment. Or we could work with what we had. There *was* soil there. A little hard to reach, but it was there, and it was ours. We could wish that soil was different or we could listen to it, understand it, tend it and trust that it was possible to grow something in it. We could condemn it as worthless for our purposes, or we could honour its potential and see where that took us. With some reluctance we took the latter path.

It was a great lesson, a powerful metaphor. Communities are the soil in which we do all the work of our vocation. If we fail to listen to that soil, understand it, love it, nurture it, feed it and work with it, we will always default into imposing, mastering and exploiting it. The world is losing the precious resource of soil at an alarming rate. Around 25 per cent of the world's soil is now severely degraded. It is estimated that 30 football fields of soil are lost every minute due to degradation.[55] Pressures on land and on soil, increasing with the effects of climate change and population growth, give rise to short-term, unsustainable farming methods which result in soil degradation. Pledging ourselves to the walls, however, is a rejection of the same short-termism in the field of mission and a commitment to discover the divine richness of the raw material we have been called to work with. As Eugene Peterson has said, 'Like the farmer with his topsoil, I must respect and honour and reverence it, be in awe before the vast mysteries contained in its unassuming ordinariness.'[56]

We can only be who we are; that is enough. The place to which we are called, with all its beauty, brokenness, potential and poverty, is truly the holy ground where we are called to nurture something of the kingdom of God. It too is enough. Rowan Williams says, 'Where we are and who we are is the furnace where the Son of God walks.'[57] The truest action of our lives is not doing *that* thing, that great thing, something truly heroic and (let's face it) truly unrealistic and magical. The truest action of our Christian lives, as we seek to wrestle with the ordinariness, or extraordinariness (usually both), of our vocation is to do *this* thing, in *this* place, with *this* community of people, that we believe with all our heart and soul we are called to do.

6

On the threshold of grace

We throw open our doors to God and discover at the same moment that he has already thrown open his door to us.

ROMANS 5:2 (MSG)

The Lord answered, 'What right do you have to be angry?'

JONAH 4:4 (GNT)

By the beginning of chapter 4 one of the key questions of the book of Jonah has been resolved. At the outset of Jonah's journey we wondered what would happen to Nineveh. By the end of chapter 3 the Ninevites have repented and God has relented from the destruction that had been threatened. However, there still remains the question of what will happen to Jonah.

At this point we could be forgiven for thinking that Jonah is a reformed character. We might reasonably be expecting a very different response from him than the one described. His vow of commitment from within the whale (Jonah 2:9) has then been followed by an obedient response to the reiteration of God's call to preach in Nineveh. So, just when it seems as though all has been resolved, there is one last twist in the tale. The narrator tells us that 'God saw what they did and how they turned from their evil ways', and responded with mercy (3:10). By contrast, Jonah sees all that God has done and how he has turned from the destruction he had promised, and is absolutely furious. Seeking to understand Jonah's fury, both towards what happens to Nineveh and towards what happens to the curious plant outside it, can help us to tease out answers, not so much to the question 'What will happen to Jonah?' as 'What is happening *in* Jonah?'

Losing our illusions

Why is Jonah angry? Though the narrator doesn't spell it out, his inventive wordplay focuses on the likely reason. The Hebrew word *ra'* is a favourite of the writer. It has been used to describe the *evil* of the Ninevites (Jonah 3:8). The same word is then used when the Ninevites 'turned from their *evil* ways' (3:10) and again when referring to God's decision to withdraw the *destruction (ra'ah)* he had threatened. By contrast, all this was literally *ra'* to Jonah 'and he became angry' (4:1). Only a seriously inattentive reader would fail to miss what the writer is trying to do. Jonah's anger is directly related to the merciful action of God. For Jonah, the *ra'* of the Ninevites should logically result in the *ra'ah* of God—when it doesn't, he is consumed by it himself.

Anger does, however, take Jonah to prayer. Where once he might have run off the scene as fast as possible, there is now a willingness to take his inner turmoil to God. And in this we are given the clearest statement of the book on the reasons for Jonah's disobedience. He fled to Tarshish because he knew God to be 'gracious and compassionate… slow to anger and abounding in love, a God who relents from sending calamity' (Jonah 4:2). Well, of course Jonah knew that. This phrase is distilled from the Hebrew scripture. Much as in the psalm from within the whale, Jonah naturally expresses his understanding of God in the language of his religious background. Only this time, as he utters the same words, he recognises that they have collided with the limits of his own assumptions. Repeating those words in the safety and security of Israel was one thing, but applying them to the Ninevites was another. Jonah confesses that at the very moment that God asked him to preach to the Ninevites he recognised that this creed was going to threaten his world view: a world where Israel was the recipient of God's love, compassion and mercy—and not anyone else. If the loving, compassionate, forgiving nature of God applied to a people as evidently wicked as the Ninevites, if this was the universe he was being asked now to live in, he would rather throw in his ticket. He cannot conceive of living in such a world. Consequently, he asks to be rid of it. He asks to die (4:3).

At this point in the Hebrew text there is a mark inviting the reader to pause. Jonah's request to die is certainly shocking, coming from the lips of a prophet. But once again the writer has slowed things down deliberately to ask us to reflect. Are we any different from Jonah? Are we not just as prone to simplifying our own world into good and bad, righteous and evil, us and them? Are we not just as susceptible to making God in our own image, employing him for our own ends? What would it feel like to have our nice neat and tidy theological universe shattered? Would it not feel like dying?

Death and anger are closely related here. Jonah sensibly takes himself out of the scene, builds himself a shelter and waits for what will happen to Nineveh. He may be trying to flee God once again, but he should know by now that that is an impossibility. God follows him to the edge of the city and provides a vine. Jonah's mood radically improves because of the vine, but then God provides a worm to destroy it and, just for good measure, a searing hot east wind to expose Jonah to the heat of the sun so severely that he begins to faint. Framing these events we hear the question from God to Jonah, 'What right do you have to be angry?' About the Ninevites? About the vine? To which Jonah replies, 'I have every right to be angry—angry enough to die' (Jonah 4:4, 9, GNT).

Jonah's words, compared with God's mercy for the Ninevites and the life and demise of something as apparently trivial as a vine, seem petulant, even childish. Comedy is certainly a feature of this wonderfully creative book, and Jonah is at times the comic anti-hero, a kind of Forrest Gump figure who is the passive object of God's dramatic interventions yet who somehow triumphs despite his incompetence. Such a figure we love and laugh at from a distance. It is satire. But like the best satire it digs at some deep questions and profound dilemmas.

For where else do death and anger work together so overtly and so powerfully as in the journey of grief? We may laugh at Jonah's tantrum, but this is a passionate protest at the dying of much of what Jonah has built his life around until now. Jonah is grieving. His world has shattered. The astute reader, the attentive member of the audience, will turn from laughter at the crumbling of Jonah's world to lament at the implications for our own.

The journey of grief is the journey of letting go as a new world, though shadowed by the loss of someone or something we held dear, comes into being. Jonah's journey has been a gradual loss of his illusions. It has been a series of events and circumstances that, by God's provision and intervention, have first made Jonah aware of the limitations of his world view and then loosened his grip on the illusions that were propping it up.

Monk and writer Thomas Keating speaks of the three fundamental emotional resources needed for happiness and well-being. These are three desires: a desire for power and control, a desire for safety and security, and a desire for esteem and affirmation.[58] Our lives are a search for the satisfaction of these fundamental desires. So often we find a kind of temporary satisfaction in our external activities, particularly those of our work or our achievements. Jonah had created a world of power, safety and esteem in his former life. He had influence; the ear of the king, who implemented his advice; the protection of the king; and the admiration and deference that came from his office and his achievements. But these were ultimately all an illusion. They disappeared the moment he headed for Joppa, and what we have been reading is the story of the 'death' of Jonah. In a sense, Jonah has been dead for a while; it's only now that he admits it.

Any structure of control, security and identity that is based primarily on our own efforts is doomed to failure. It is insufficient. Sooner or later it will find us out. Sooner or later something or someone will burst the bubble of that world. All spirituality is learning to die. Or put another way, all true spirituality is learning to grasp the life-through-death that Jesus offers. It is learning to travel the paradoxical journey through death towards the life that Jesus offers. It is to trust the truth of Jesus' statements:

Whoever loses their life for my sake will find it. (Matthew 10:39)

Whoever wants to be my disciple must deny themselves and take up their cross and follow me. (Mark 8:34)

Anyone who loves their life will lose it, while anyone who hates their life in this world will keep it for eternal life. (John 12:25)

All spirituality is unlearning the lie of the illusions of our own petty attempts at control, security and status and learning to embrace the truth of God's universe—a universe where there is only one God and it's not us, or some sham of a king, idol or god we have installed in God's place.

On the floor of Jonah's booth, that rather pathetic temporary structure of his own making, a final effort at self-provision, lies the shattered remains of a world that must be left behind. It is a place that feels like death and failure. Yet it is the very foundation of life.

Sometimes I sense that we expect our growth to be a consistent journey upwards, towards greater holiness, greater effectiveness, greater intimacy with God. But it seldom looks like that or feels like that. Spiritual growth cannot take that trajectory. And that trajectory is not modelled to us or offered to us by Jesus. We are invited to die in order to live, to descend in order to rise. We are not in the world of sales figures or the stock market. The economy of the kingdom is not built on endless accumulation but on radical sacrifice. Our growth comes by dying, the painful loss of structures, assumptions, dreams and convictions that we thought were the source of life. It is God alone, not an expression of him, or a ministry for him, that is the source of life. His ultimate desire is for us to place all our fundamental desires within the scope of his love for us, within the scope of his care. It is to invite God, and him alone, to inhabit the centre of our constellation of needs and hopes and allow them to orientate themselves around him. To do that requires a willingness to let go, to recognise our illusions for what they are and allow them to be evicted from the centre and replaced by God himself.

Unfurling grace

Throughout this whole journey God has been holding out an invitation to Jonah: an invitation to live, truly live, in a universe beyond the illusions of his own sense of control, security and identity and within a world resting on the truth that it is God who is in control, God who provides ultimate security, God who affirms who we are. The invitation is to let go of the attachment to false idols, illusory gods that masquerade as the true God, and to attach himself fully to the Lord God alone. It is the invitation to recognise what feel like important, often life-giving attachments to be as nothing compared with the ultimate attachment of trust in Jesus. We are invited by Jesus to 'leave everything' and 'follow me', to give our primary love and faithfulness to Jesus and allow all others to find their place in deference to him. It is the invitation therefore to a new kind of reality created by dying to self, dying with Christ and rising to a new life where the life-giving centre is Christ.

In the Gospels Jesus calls this eternal life. He also calls it the kingdom of God. Paul calls it salvation; he also calls it grace. Jonah is being invited to continue his life and vocation in this new reality beyond that created by his own illusions. He is being invited to embrace the maturing of his own life and vocation more and more within a deeper reality, where the God of Israel is also the Lord of all creation. It means that, for Jonah, the journey does not end, though the story does. And nor does it end for us—we are constantly invited 'further up and further in',[59] invited to journey ever onwards to inhabit ever more fully the resulting reality of our acceptance of Jesus' call. Eternal life, salvation, grace is an unfolding reality into which we are constantly being invited to journey ever deeper.

This is how Paul describes this journey:

> Therefore, since we have been justified through faith, we have peace with God through our Lord Jesus Christ, through whom we

have gained access by faith into this grace in which we now stand.
ROMANS 5:1–2

At first glance this description of grace seems a little static. We might imagine 'gaining access' into a new world and being given a place 'in which we now stand' as filling a new square, achieving a new status. However, the Greek word which is translated 'gained access' has the sense of being introduced, much like a suitor to a king, or a guest to a function. The implication is much more of an initiative on the part of God which we are invited to participate in.

The implication is also one of movement: of a threshold being revealed, of a new world being made accessible to us. It is the invitation to cross over and to step into that world and journey onwards, to explore it, enjoy it, breathe its air and live in its environment.

The paraphrase translation *THE MESSAGE* captures this sense of movement beautifully:

We throw open our doors to God and discover at the same moment that he has already thrown open his door to us.
ROMANS 5:2, MSG

There is not only a sense of movement, but also an affirmation of God's initiative. We are invited to see God almost playfully creating space just ahead of us, just out of sight, as though laying a delicious trail for us out of the woods and into the clearing. But the clearing is just the beginning—God continues to move on, beckoning us further. It is a description of the kind of world we have been invited into. In this world, at almost the same moment as we take the initiative to accept God's grace, we realise that we are in fact accepting a prior invitation by God himself. It is as though the ground of this new world opens up before us just at the moment we commit to stepping forward. The world of grace is an unfolding one, an unfurling one, where the next instalment, the next chapter, is always opening up just ahead of us and beckoning us towards it.

In his hastily constructed booth, on the edge of Nineveh, as he waits stubbornly for God to act in one way or another, Jonah is on the threshold of grace. The deconstructed illusions of his life of active, assertive success lie about him like wasted betting slips, or worthless stock market shares. As he looks beyond the threshold towards the grace he is being invited to live in, he must ask what it truly means to be human, what it means to carry out his vocation in a world where status, identity and purpose emerge from losing control rather than constantly fighting to gain it.

In this world of unfurling grace the relationship between our initiative and God's is a mysterious one. When our world was governed by our illusions of control, security and status this relationship was rather more straightforward. It was our own energy, enterprise and effort that moved us forward, nothing else. But is the world of grace a world where we live in passive service to the initiative and activity of God? Having lived lives of active assertion, do we convert to lives of passivity? We know this is not true, and it certainly does not feel like that. When God calls us he calls us to action, to participation and to co-operation with him. So what is the relationship between our action and that of God's? What does it mean to live in grace, beyond the damaging dominance of our own assertiveness, and within the reign of the lordship of Christ? Furthermore, what does it mean to lead and minister as people of grace? How do we lead as wounded people who have learnt through pain and loss that our own attempts at control and success have proved woefully insufficient?

Finding our middle voice

These are questions that have been simmering gently throughout the book of Jonah and which now come to a climax as the book closes. The author invited us to ask at the story's outset, 'What will happen to Jonah?' He now asks, 'And what will happen now that his illusion of control has disappeared?' How will Jonah and God's actions relate to one another now? There is an exchange of both words and action, a give-and-take of statement and question, action and counteraction, as Jonah wrestles with God. Jonah makes a shelter. God provides a vine. Jonah is happy about this. God provides a worm which withers the vine. Then God provides a dry, hot east wind to wither Jonah himself. Jonah vents his anger. God challenges Jonah's anger. Jonah asserts it all the more. Whereas, previously, whole sections of the story have flowed from the actions or words of God or Jonah, now the narrative is like a final showdown, a physical and verbal contest of increasing intensity. We await the result. We expect closure. We read on for the take-home message, a final and satisfying resolution.

Except, of course, there is no resolution. Only a final question:

> But the Lord said, 'You have been concerned about this plant, though you did not tend it or make it grow. It sprang up overnight and died overnight. And should I not have concern for the great city of Nineveh, in which there are more than a hundred and twenty thousand people who cannot tell their right hand from their left—and also many animals?'
> JONAH 4:10–11

The end. No conclusion. Just another question. But it is a question designed to take the reader to a place of reflection once more. It is designed to unsettle our assumptions about what we think we know about the ways of God's grace and mercy. If God can be as concerned with unpredictable vines, herds of cattle and ignorant Ninevites as he is with the people of Israel then this grace and mercy is a far more wild, unpredictable and mysterious thing than we had ever realised. The ground beneath our feet is far less sure than we imagined. We thought we understood the mind of God and now we're not so sure. We thought we knew how to navigate this landscape, now we're not sure we'll ever venture out again.

Throughout my experience of missional leadership in Poole, this has been a live question. From the beginning we were committed to seeking to listen to what God's initiative might be—where was he calling us? Where was he already at work and inviting us to participate? At the same time, along with others in our community, I brought some gifts of creativity, imagination and strategic planning to mission too. How could these cooperate with God's mission? How could I discern whether these were serving the mission we were leading or beginning to drive it?

At points I have reached a place not dissimilar to Jonah's, simply wanting to throw in the towel, confused by the apparent fickleness and unpredictability of God. On a number of occasions things had taken a very different course from the one we had expected, for reasons I could not explain. On other occasions it felt as if our efforts were working hard to keep up with what God was doing. I constantly wrestled with the mystery of how my efforts and God's initiative related. Then on one particular occasion a significant piece of work, which had consumed a huge amount of energy and dedication, came to a close in a way that was humbling for all involved.

The café in which much of our mission and ministry had started and grown had become a community café which we ran for three years. The decision to take on a licence to run the café for ourselves at the heart of Poole's High Street was not one we had taken lightly. I personally agonised over the decision, had a good number of sleepless nights, and sought earnestly God's voice on the decision. However, with each tentative step towards gathering the resources needed even to begin such a venture it seemed that God provided, at points quite miraculously. We were willing to take risks and embrace possible failure in doing so. At the time, as I stood between equally rational choices of taking a risk or playing safe, I was struck powerfully by a verse from Ecclesiastes:

Whoever watches the wind will not plant;
whoever looks at the clouds will not reap.
ECCLESIASTES 11:4

There was never going to be a perfect time to take such a risk. We had been given an opportunity, an open door; we could choose to venture in, or not. Either way, God was with us.

So we ventured in. Running the café was exhilarating and challenging, frustrating and also immensely rewarding. It was, however, ultimately unsustainable, both financially and in terms of people's energy and resources. After three years of trying to find a solution to these issues we reluctantly but unanimously agreed to bring the project to a close. At the end we held a celebration party, at the conclusion of which I stood up to say a few words. I looked out at about 75 people who had all been intimately involved with the café, at least half of whom were not connected to the church or Christian faith in any other way. Each person I looked out on had a story to tell about the impact the café had had on them; each person had been embraced by the community of that café and changed by it. It was a proud moment. It was a holy moment.

Having said that, the necessary decision to allow that project to die posed a very profound question in me. I reached a point of real dilemma. It was a crisis of confidence in my own ability to discern God's voice. But it was also a theological crisis, a sense that I did not know any more on what basis to understand the relationship between my action and God's. I looked back on that decision three years before. How much of my own drive, my own desire to seize the initiative, had influenced the decision to take that project on? Or was it not also true that a door had opened for that initiative to take flight? Had not God opened that door and invited us in?

Thankfully I rediscovered a beautiful insight from Eugene Peterson in his book *The Contemplative Pastor*. He points out that whereas English only has two voices, active and passive, Greek has three. These are active voice, passive voice and a third, or 'middle', voice. In the active voice I am the subject of the action; I take the initiative. In the passive voice I am the object of an action; I experience or am affected in some way by the initiative of another. However, with the middle voice I am a subject that participates in the action that another has initiated. Not only am I participating but I choose to participate; I actively participate in an action that is the result of the initiative of another.

Peterson relates this insight to the distinctiveness of Christian prayer. Whereas pagan prayer involves active rituals aimed at rousing a passive god from slumber, and other forms of prayer, particularly Hindu prayer, aim at a passive reception of the will and action of the gods, Christian prayer is about entering into the ongoing action and grace of God. In prayer we lift our voice to join with what has already been begun by God. In Christian prayer:

> We neither manipulate God (active voice) nor are manipulated by God (passive voice). We are involved in the action and participate in its results but do not define it (middle voice). Prayer takes place in the middle voice.[60]

What is true of prayer is true of all of life within the world of unfurling grace that God invites us ever more deeply into. We die to a need of control which can result in manipulation of others and God. But what takes the place of that desire is not nothing, resulting in a meaningless passivity. The space we are invited to inhabit is one where we willingly participate in the flow of action that has resulted from the gracious initiative of God.

At the time of my own crisis I began to hear this message from various and unexpected sources. The seeds of this book were planted during a few days I spent at a monastery in Surrey. I sought the counsel of an experienced monk there and spent an hour relating the details of my increasingly fragile illusions to him. After listening to my ramblings patiently he responded by saying very simply, 'I think you need to go with the flow a bit more.' This was not, as you might think, an encouragement towards a relaxed passivity. I took it as a call to a greater attentiveness to the flow of God's Spirit and a counsel to have the courage to let go and let that flow take me.

Some months later I watched the film *Boyhood* (2014), a coming-of-age film which follows the childhood and adolescence of one boy. The passive attitude of the boy is contrasted with the driven attitude of his mother as she tries to make something of her life. While he seems to drift aimlessly through school she retrains as a college teacher to ensure that she can provide for her family as a single mother. Her son cuts a figure of benign apathy, yet one who seems happy. Meanwhile she moves from one unhappy relationship to another. At the end of the film, the boy leaves home for the first time and goes to college. He falls easily into the company of a group of fellow freshers as they arrive and together they head away from the urgency of student parties and into the desert outside the city. As the film closes there is an exchange between the boy and a girl student he has just met. The girl says to him, 'You know how people say "Seize the moment"? Do you ever wonder if it's actually the other way round—the moment seizes you?'

I also listened to Brother Sam, the warden of a Franciscan community in the heart of Dorset, speak about his experience of monastic life. I asked him to come to speak to a group of people from some of the workplaces in Poole about what lessons the monastic life might have to offer to the world of work. 'Not many,' he said mischievously! And then he talked compellingly about the countercultural but utterly life-giving gospel values that inform and energise the community he leads. And in teasing out the commitment to obedience as opposed to ambition he said, almost as an aside, 'You know some of the best decisions of my life have been made *for* me.'

The journey of Jonah is a journey from the active voice of Jonah's former life towards the middle voice of that willed participation in the action of God. When the logical limitations of Jonah's active-voice life and ministry are laid bare, Jonah perhaps thinks the only alternative is passivity. Unable to bear the thought of such a life he cries out, 'It is better for me to die than to live!' (Jonah 4:3). But God's final question invites Jonah, and us, to consider a third way, a middle voice which opens up a very different kind of world. A world where we allow ourselves to be seized rather than forever to strive to take control. A world where we need not assert our own decisiveness but lean into the decision of others. A liberating world where we can choose to enter into the flow of action which has its origins in the gracious mercy and compassion of God. A world of unfurling grace where we willingly participate in the rhythm and flow of God's initiative and God's work.

7

Stepping into grace:
the contemplative life

> The chief actor in the historic mission of the Christian Church is the Holy Spirit… This fact, so patent to Christians in the first century, is largely forgotten in our own. So we have lost our nerve and our sense of direction and turned the divine initiative into a human enterprise.
>
> BISHOP J.V. TAYLOR[61]

> Jonah had gone out and sat down at a place east of the city. There he made himself a shelter, sat in its shade and waited…
>
> JONAH 4:5

What hope is there for Jonah as his story comes to an end? With no resolution to Jonah's predicament, are we meant to assume that he lived out his days as a religious tourist attraction on the edge of Nineveh? A ridiculous discard of a prophet desperately tending his booth, a symbol of the wreckage of his former life? Is he left in our imaginations as a salutary figure warning of the consequences of a vision too narrow to include the vastness of the grace of God? Perhaps.

I do not sense the narrator of Jonah is simply offering this tale of a prophet in order to create a sort of scapegoat character for the dangers of religious narrow-mindedness. The book of Jonah may certainly contain imaginative and creative elements, but its foundations are in the realities of the life of Israel. Jonah was not a nobody; he was somebody, located in time and place. So while Jonah's story may be made outlandish and dramatic enough for him to be made an example of, it is also real and human enough for him to be an example *for* us.

So there is hope in the story of Jonah and not least in his reaction to witnessing the shattering of his vision. When Jonah's rehabilitation and recommitment do not bring about the judgement of Nineveh that he predicted they would, Jonah does not completely leave the scene. Instead he remains, stubbornly, on the edge of it. He is angry, disappointed, broken. But he is still there. And still praying to his

God. And in this book of structures and limitations, where Jonah has journeyed from one container of his hopes and dreams to another, his final move involves the construction of one last, flimsy, feeble shelter. The shelter symbolises his brokenness and his desperation, the reality of the deconstruction of all the false structures that have propped him up in the past. But it is also a shelter that signifies the beginning of new life.

For the beginning of learning to live in the world of grace, which God invites us into, comes in ceasing to be at the centre of events, ceasing always to have to be part of the action, ceasing to exert our power or agenda. Learning to live in the world of grace involves learning to wait, often at the edge of things, and above all else waiting patiently and being attentive to what God will do. This is not an easy place. It may well feel as alienating, useless and exposed a place as Jonah's booth must have felt to him. But it is the place we need to cultivate and maintain in order to inhabit this world of grace.

Understanding the importance of this space, learning how to nurture it and maintain it, is, I believe, a crucial task for the development of our vocational and spiritual lives. In this space we practise what it means to let go of those illusions of control, security and identity and we learn to yield all that we are into the presence of God. In this space we are voluntarily vulnerable so as to make ourselves open to the love and presence of God. We lay aside our future-oriented agendas, concerns, strategies and dreams and are deliberately attentive simply to God as he is, not what we might want him to be, or do for us.

The traditions of the Church have a word for this—it is called contemplation. It has been central to Christian formation and spiritual growth for centuries but in recent centuries has been exiled, kept alive predominantly by the monastic orders. It has been regarded as a monastic practice, and made liable to the prejudices of taste and churchmanship, rather than being understood as a fundamental way of Christian life. Thankfully, the contemplative tradition is finding traction again. It is doing so because its vitality is real and orthodox. But it is doing so also because we as Christian individuals, communities and institutions are finding ourselves increasingly in the bewildered place of Jonah's booth, exhausted by driven endeavour, and searching for another way to be Christian ministers and leaders in a foreign land.

What is contemplation?

First of all let's be clear what contemplation is not. It is not the practice of certain techniques of prayer or stillness. It is not just the name for a Christian mindfulness: 'Contemplation is a way of living, beholding and wondering before it is a way of praying.'[62] Prayer, perhaps certain kinds of prayer, may well be part of its landscape, but this is to confuse the part with the whole. Nor is contemplation simply reflective practice or thoughtfulness. Again, a willed attentiveness and reflectiveness on ourselves and the world around us may well be part of contemplation but it is not the whole. There are a great many practices and exercises that have become important or helpful in exploring contemplation, but these are not the essence of what contemplation is. We need to distinguish between contemplative practice and the contemplative life. Contemplative practices are part of contemplation in that they help nurture and establish the experience and attitude of contemplation. But contemplation is not an ambition, something we can strive or work towards by our own efforts and the strict application of certain disciplines.

For at its heart, contemplation is a gift, the gift of grace and the gift of a growing experience in the world of grace. The contemplative *life*, to make a distinction from contemplative *practice*, is a life alive to the wonder of the presence of God in us and in all creation. It is fundamentally inspired by the truth that God is already present in us and already present in creation. For this reason, writers from the contemplative tradition speak of the contemplative life as 'awareness', of a deepening recognition of God's presence in the world and in the moment. They also speak of a cultivated 'attentiveness' so as to behold and apprehend this presence in ourselves and in the world.

Contemplation is life 'beyond' self, beyond our selfish concerns and the masquerades of the ego, which is why the contemplative life cannot simply be willed on our part. The journey into deeper contemplation will almost certainly involve darkness, periods of confusion and struggle that are part of the work of God in loosening our grip on our own efforts at control. Contemplation is something we begin to feel is 'happening' to us as we begin to rest in the reality of God. Hence, the contemplative life is one where we find it possible to turn our attention more deeply towards God, our true self and the world.

Yet the contemplative life is not passive! It is letting go and letting God, but not then letting ourselves lapse into inactivity. Instead, the contemplative life roots action in the context of an intimate relationship with God. This relationship invites participation on the basis of liberation, liberation from our attempts at knowing and asserting that knowledge in the world. The contemplative life is founded upon a relationship of love with God purely for God's sake. It is a life that begins with a letting go of any move to use God for our own aims, import him into our plans, mine our knowledge of him for our own ends. It is love of God for God's sake.

Contemplative action is rooted in relationship, in the *person* of God, not what we think we know *about* God. This is a knowledge that goes beyond intellectual faculties, through experience and ultimately towards a union with God where we touch God's fundamental being: who he is, just for who he is. Our action emerges on the basis of our relationship with God, not our intellectual information on God. Writer and Trappist monk Thomas Merton said:

> Contemplation... is... a religious and transcendent gift. It is not something to which we can attain alone, by intellectual effort, by perfecting our natural powers. It is not a kind of self-hypnosis, resulting from concentration on our own inner spiritual being. It is not the fruit of our own efforts. It is the gift of God who, in his mercy, completes the hidden and mysterious work of creation in us by enlightening our hearts and minds, by awakening in us

the awareness that we are words spoken in his one Word, and the creating Spirit dwells in us and we in him. That we are 'in Christ' and that Christ lives in us. That the natural life in us has been completed, elevated, transformed and fulfilled in Christ by his Holy Spirit. Contemplation is the awareness and realisation, even in some sense experience, of what each Christian obscurely believes: 'It is no longer I that live but Christ lives in me.'[63]

The contemplative Jesus

When we look at the life of Jesus we see a model of the contemplative life. Jesus radically and controversially claimed to know God as a Father; he claimed to have a relationship with God in this incredible, intimate way. The dynamic in the Gospels between Jesus and the Pharisees reflects this fundamental clash between the Pharisees' limited understanding of the knowledge of God and Jesus' invitation to know God through relationship. Jesus' anger with the Pharisees is not so much towards their error but towards their turning of an error into a dogma, a dogma that was used as a means of ostracising and abusing the vulnerable.

Jesus warns his disciples of the 'yeast of the Pharisees' (Matthew 16:11, Mark 8:15, Luke 12:1). This yeast is the creeping tendency in the human ego to domesticise God. To say that what we know about God is the way God is. And then to become master and keeper of that knowledge, controlling and abusing people with it.

Jesus the contemplative invites us to venture beyond any limitation of the knowledge of God and to begin to know God infinitely through relationship. In any relationship of intimacy we do not describe our knowledge of someone fundamentally through prosaic description—it will never do them justice. Poetry gets us a little closer. But really that kind of knowledge goes beyond description, beyond knowing at all. Contemplation 'sees "without seeing" and knows "without knowing"'.[64]

What Jesus models for us is a life that is committed to living from the well of that relational knowledge. Such knowledge can only begin to spring up through death to the illusions of our own knowledge, our own control, our own security and identity. Jesus' first 'death', in a sense, is in the wilderness when the devil tests Jesus' commitment to a life based on a relationship with the Father. Jesus emerges from the desert 'in the power of the Spirit' (Luke 4:14), fully alive to the well-spring of life flowing from a relationship of intimacy with God the Father.

Contemplatives will point to the pictures of Jesus retreating from the intense demands of ministry to be with his Father in quiet and solitude (Luke 5:16). This is how Jesus maintains this relationship upon which all his visible action is based. While prayer and worship remain part of the communal life he is establishing with the disciples, the critical element of private, hidden prayer to the Father is modelled to us. And it is this practice that maintains a constant awareness of the presence and action of the Father as Jesus goes about his ministry. Jesus can 'do only what he sees his Father doing' (John 5:19) and speaks not only on the basis of a thorough knowledge of scripture but also from 'what I have seen in the Father's presence' (John 8:38). We see in the life of Jesus a life utterly liberated from any attachment to a limiting knowledge of God and utterly liberated to be spent in the constant presence and awareness of God the Father.

Practising attentiveness

Contemplation is a gift. It is the gift of relationship with God beyond knowing. Inhabiting that relationship is the work of a lifetime; it is what Paul refers to when he urges the Philippians to 'continue to work out your salvation with fear and trembling' (Philippians 2:12). Venturing further into the world of grace into which Jesus invites us is ultimately God's work in us (Philippians 2:13). But it is a work in which we are invited to participate. The 'middle voice' ministry I described in the last chapter is accompanied by a 'middle voice spirituality'. Our spirituality becomes less about asserting our needs, wants and desires to God than about listening and cultivating attentiveness to God. It is a willed participation in a life which has been initiated by the Father.

Silence and prayer based on a wordless attentiveness to God, what many call contemplative prayer, has more and more become the essential basis of prayer for me. And it has opened up a whole world of attentiveness in every other area of life. An alarmingly simple commitment to base my life and ministry on a quiet desire to rest on God, with no agenda, no words, no noise, purely for his sake, has opened up huge areas of growth in the awareness of God in the world.

I liken it to when I started birdwatching. People think birdwatching is a hobby. It's far more serious than that! Birdwatching is something I can no longer switch on and off. Of course, there are trips and visits that I go on that are for the purpose of birdwatching. But really I am always birdwatching. Birdwatching has become part of life, birds a constant presence—because birdwatching is a training in attentiveness.

I took up birdwatching ten years ago. A counsellor I was seeing at the time asked me about life outside work. The reality was that at that stage in my life time for interests that had previously sustained me was being squeezed out. 'So why not take up something else?' she asked. 'What would you do if you decided to do something you've never done?' So I began birdwatching with a cheap pair of sports binoculars, and it was one of the best decisions I've ever made.

Perhaps the greatest revelation in my growing passion for birdwatching was the world that opened up to me when I began to learn the songs and calls of birds. Identifying birds by sight is a great way of birdwatching but identifying them by call opens things up radically. I fairly quickly learnt most of the calls of common birds. Then I invested in some CDs and online materials that helped me learn a whole host of others, particularly the calls of birds that are difficult to see, or all look the same!

Suddenly the background audio world of birds that lies there unobtrusively but consistently in even the most 'unwild' of environments began to reveal its secrets. It was like learning a new language. Like switching to shortwave radio and suddenly discovering a foreign station making sense. It was as though this dimension of wilderness that had seemed so distant and mysterious had crept closer and I was party to its presence while others carried on obliviously. It was a transforming discovery. For me, learning birdsong opened up a world that helped me reconnect with the wonder and diversity of the natural world that had been there all the time if only I had stopped to listen. It also helped me enhance my ability to forget myself and my petty concerns and pay attention to something else.

And the point is this: I spent time, energy and a certain amount of money on training materials to help me learn this new kind of attentiveness. Learning the difference between a reed warbler and a sedge warbler calling from the depths of a reed bed takes time and practice. Now I can do it almost instantaneously. In the same way, training yourself in attentiveness to the hidden presence of God in his creation takes time, energy and dedication. But it can be done. When we start to practise forms of prayer that emphasise a wordless, agenda-less attentiveness to God himself, we begin to notice him everywhere.

Furthermore, in the same way that birdwatching for me became a practice of self-forgetting, of recognising my own small place in the wonder of creation, contemplative prayer, the practice of a simple stillness before God, trains us in reorientation. Our vocation and ministry do place us at times at the centre of things. They certainly place us at the centre of our own schedules and our own concerns. My prayer life at times simply became an extension of this perspective as I fervently sought God to attend to the weight of my own anxieties. Gradually, I have learnt to be with God for his sake alone and find in the process my agenda being gently scaled down to its proper proportions in the light of his presence.

Essentially what we are doing in contemplative prayer is practising vulnerability. We are willingly participating in our own vulnerability so that we might willingly participate in the transforming initiative of God at work in us day by day. Vulnerability, as I discussed before, is the key to intimacy, the key to relationships of real depth and authenticity. Vulnerability is also the key to wholeheartedness, to living life to the full, because only in allowing ourselves to be found by others just for who we are, not who we might pretend or imagine ourselves to be, do we base our lives on the kinds of relationship that enable us to thrive. Contemplative prayer is a practised vulnerability with God, a letting go of our pretences, masks and illusory facades to come before God just for who he is. Worship can do this. Experiences of the Holy Spirit can do this. Contemplative prayer seeks to establish a space for maintaining this practised vulnerability in daily life.

There is a paradox contained in all of this. Contemplation is a gift, a gift of grace as God deepens our relationship with him. But we can be active in participating in this process. I am reminded of the opening of Derek Mahon's wonderful poem 'A Disused Shed in Co. Wexford'. Mahon describes coming across an old shed deep 'in the grounds of a burnt-out old hotel/among the bathtubs and the wash basins'. Looking through the keyhole of the door he discovers in the darkness inside a bloom of white mushrooms. The poem opens with the line, 'Even now there are places where a thought might grow.'[65] In the same way, contemplative prayer is about creating the sort of space, beyond the clutter and noise of everyday life, where attentiveness to God's presence might grow. Contemplative prayer is about willingly seeking to make our soul the kind of place where God's presence may spring up in us. It is about opening and offering spaces amid the confusion and clamour of life, the kind of quiet, unbusy, remote spaces that will allow our relationship with God—whom we cannot truly know, but can only allow to be known in us—to grow.

Movements in the contemplative life

To reiterate, the practice of contemplation must not be confused with the contemplative life. What I mean by the latter is a life where our primary relationship with God the Father is allowed to inform and influence every other area of life. It is a life of participation in grace, in the invitation to venture deeper into grace, which itself is an unfurling of God's presence in time and space. In the contemplative life we seek to model our life on Jesus, whose contemplative practice of spending time in lonely and withdrawn places was the basis for a life which sought continually to participate in what the Father had already initiated.

What might the contemplative life begin to look like? I think it can be described as four key movements. These movements are the outward expression of transformation taking place at the level of the soul. Once again we cannot *make* such transformation occur and in some cases only processes like those of the dark night can bring about the sort of transformation needed. However, we can wilfully participate in them when we begin to notice them. We can lean into what will feel, initially anyway, like very uncomfortable changes in us and our responses to the world around us.

From hurry to hospitality

Hurry is a symptom of a soul that is sick. We hurry when we are at the centre of our own universe, when we become convinced that only our actions and our endeavour can achieve all that needs to be achieved. We believe ourselves to be indispensable; we may not admit to this, but we act as though it were true. Hurry is an expression of 'functional atheism'.[66] We may believe that God is the creator and sustainer of the universe but our actions suggest completely the opposite.

Jesus told many agrarian parables. He did this partly because this was the world he inhabited, but also because they illustrate a fundamental truth about the world of grace. Agriculture is a creative participation in a natural process which is being sustained by God. So it is with the world of grace. Jesus tells us that this world of grace is like a farmer who sows seed on the ground: 'Night and day, whether he sleeps or gets up, the seed sprouts and grows, *though he does not know how*' (Mark 4:27, emphasis mine). The picture is of a farmer participating in a process far bigger and more mysterious than he can fathom. He does not seek to control this process; he is humble before its mystery. He trusts the mystery of this process so much that he can welcome sleep rather than maintain an anxious and impatient vigilance over his project. He is content that the harvest will ultimately come 'all by itself' (Mark 4:28). However, he is by no means idle. He is continually discerning how and when to participate in this mysterious divine process.

The picture is of a life and ministry free from hurry and free from anxiety, a life that submits humbly to rhythms and processes that have their initiative in the creativity of God. In that sense the role of the farmer, the participant in the life of God, is one of welcome. It is about making space, providing a home for this creative, life-giving power from God. The word I would use is 'hospitality'.

Hospitality describes exactly that active participation in life as it *comes to us*. Hospitality is not simply welcome; it is far more active and attentive than that. Hospitality is a discerned creation of the kind of environment that will enable life in all its fullness to thrive. So there is plenty of work to be done. But there is also recognition that there comes a point where no more can be done. There is day and night, work and rest. This rest is not simply for physical recuperation. Nor is it a collapsed exhaustion when every ounce of energy has been spent. It is an expression of the reality that the power at work in the kingdom, in the world of grace, is a power beyond us. We can welcome it, seek to work with it, but we cannot contain it, or manage it. Hospitality therefore signifies a deeper attitude. It is a kind of poise which guards us against anxiety and hurry, gives permission for rest without guilt, and encourages us to work creatively with God to create spaces where the life of the kingdom can grow.

From anxiety to attentiveness

One of the growing features of our driven, utilitarian culture is anxiety. Anxiety is a product of uncertainty and of fear. It is also one product of a sense of the lack of discernible structures that might offer reliable support and protection from the things we fear. Our own culture has seen an erosion of the authority of those sorts of structures in the past decades. And in recent years a series of scandals has hugely damaged trust in some of the key institutions that support and enrich our lives: Parliament, the financial sector, the media, sports institutions like FIFA and the IAAF, and the Church.

There is sadly plenty to be anxious about, with a litany of overwhelmingly challenging threats on an international scale: climate change, terrorism, pandemics, mass movements of refugees and migrants, food shortages, to name just a few. Our anxiety is reflected in our culture. For example, there has been a huge rise in the prevalence of post-apocalyptic films, films set in the context of a world beyond the global disaster that we fear.

The Christian vision, however, is one of a created universe initiated and sustained by God that is moving to a conclusion which gives us hope. The Christian hope is not for some post-apocalyptic heaven for those not 'left behind', but for a renewed heaven and earth governed and held together 'in Christ'. Furthermore, the Christian vision is one of a God who is present and active in his creation, already at work in the process of renewal since the resurrection of Jesus, and inviting us as co-carriers of his presence to participate in this amazing project.

This vision, I believe, invites us first and foremost to be people of attentiveness, people who constantly seek to discover what God is doing in the world and to participate in it. Our priority must be to keep in touch with the initiative and power of God so that we might keep in step with it. In that sense, attentiveness (discerning what God is doing) and obedience (joining in) are our key aims in pursuing our vocation and carrying out our ministry.

It is when we lose sight of this and allow other agendas and aims to take the place of attentiveness that anxiety begins to creep in. Any other agenda will be, to some extent, beyond our control. As soon as we allow it to become our top priority we are putting ourselves beyond grace and into a space which will pressurise us to assert our control and capability, and which will start to reinforce our illusions of self.

This could be said to be true of Jonah, whose agenda has also been confused. He has sought success for God, but not sought God just for the sake of who he is. The book of Jonah is a tale of the realignment of Jonah's agenda. When God asks his final question, 'Should I not have concern for the great city of Nineveh?' (Jonah 4:11), he is essentially asking Jonah, 'Do you trust me with your agenda, or not?' Unless we trust God with our agendas, we will always find them rising above the most important one—loving attention to God for his sake, not ours.

Anxiety is the ever-present wolf lurking at the door of a Church deeply concerned about its own demise and for its own future. In that climate, 'growth' is the word that seems to define the agenda for much of the Church's priorities. But growth cannot be our fundamental aim in ministry, for growth is ultimately out of our control. We can help create the kind of environments in which growth, both quantitative and qualitative, can take place, but growth itself is something that takes place 'all by itself'. If we become focused on growth alone to the exclusion of all else, we have set up an idol that may well consume us, first with anxiety and then completely.

Writing over 30 years ago, Bishop John Taylor was acutely aware of the creeping culture of success and achievement within which the Church existed. He also cited the increasing power available to the world of work in the form of new tools for communication and computing. Yet in that culture he urged the Church to remain wary of the lure of technique and method, of the enticing power that modern technology affords us. The greatest power we have, he argued, is one that was available before any of these innovations, or any since. It is the Holy Spirit. Not only that, it is the gift of the Holy Spirit as a gift, not just of power but also of sight. It is the Holy Spirit, the 'go-between God', that enables us to see, to witness and to participate in the work of the Father. Our priority, our ambition, therefore, must surely be to be attentive to the Holy Spirit with all that we are.

It is seeing, insight, that should be our focus. As Bishop Taylor said, 'The prophets and apostles were obsessed by divine revelation or the lack of it; we are obsessed by human response or the lack of it.'[67] Modern church practices—learning and disseminating techniques and models that have worked elsewhere and learning and applying lessons from other glitteringly successful fields, not least that of business—can distract us from the one thing that is necessary, the person who is a unique gift to the Church: the Holy Spirit. That gift is a gift of power, but he must also be rediscovered as a gift of seeing. We must be as wildly obsessed with revelation as the apostles and early Church were. And that means we must be obsessed by attentiveness, a desire to be attentive to the work of the Spirit, in the world, in our communities, and in that still small voice within us, asking us to join in with what he is doing.

From reactiveness to responsiveness

If reactiveness is a result of anxiety, responsiveness is the fruit of attentiveness, a fruit of the contemplative life. The opposite of contemplation is not action, but reaction.[68] Reaction is that state of mind and being that we drift into when anxiety, hurry and circumstance work their way into the centre. We find ourselves problem-solving constantly, fire-fighting one crisis after another, never really aware of what the root cause of the problem is, because we haven't found the time to discern it.

Of course, we cannot avoid having to react to circumstances and events, but it is the kind of reaction that is critical. Responsiveness is contemplative reaction, a reaction rooted in attentiveness and prayerful discernment. Responsiveness is patient, even slow, but wise, insightful and ultimately more fruitful.

In his book *Hit the Ground Kneeling*, Bishop Stephen Cottrell tells a wonderful story to illustrate the difference between these two responses. He relates his experience as a young scout at scout camp when he witnessed a friend falling 20 feet from a piece of play equipment. His friend hit the ground and lay motionless as though dead. The group of scouts ran in a state of panic to the scoutmaster to tell him what had happened. However, rather than running back to the scene of the accident, the scoutmaster walked, steadily and directly, but nevertheless with an attitude that did not convince the boys that he fully appreciated the urgency of the situation. In the end the boy was fine. But those who saw him fall were still angry with the scoutmaster for his attitude. Until, that is, he explained his response:

> He told us that he'd needed a few moments to think; he'd needed time to weigh up the situation because his first action had to be the right one... there might be no opportunity for a second action. He had also walked so that he wouldn't be out of breath if he needed to give the fallen boy mouth-to-mouth resuscitation.[69]

As it happened, mouth-to-mouth was exactly what the boy needed and the reason the boy was saved. And as it happened, this was a story that stayed with a young Stephen Cottrell and taught him something very important about the contemplative life. As he says, 'Sometimes the best leadership requires stillness and composure. Then the right decisions are taken. Then the difficult decisions are faced.'[70]

A world of great anxiety makes it harder and harder to respond with discernment rather than just simply reaction. In a world of great anxiety everything starts to look like an emergency. Likewise in the Church. Stephen Cottrell's book was given its title in response to a sense of exasperation at parish churches with leadership vacancies constantly asking for vicars who could 'hit the ground running'. What kind of ministers do we want if we demand leaders who approach ministry like an SAS special missions squad? And what kind of ministers will we be if we collude with the congregations who ask us to be like that? Yet this is what we will end up being unless we slow down enough to listen and discern the presence and action of God in our communities and contexts. This is what we will be unless we learn to attentively respond to what God is doing rather than react to the loudest voices and the most urgent crises.

From utility to humility

Finally, a life of contemplation is one that is committed to humility, to downward mobility, to becoming less, so that Christ may become greater (John 3:30). The early Church fathers talked about this in relation to the term 'self-accusation'. Self-accusation, though it sounds rather like a harsh critique of ourselves, is instead a willingness to face the truth of our frailty and our failings. It is the humility to accept ourselves, with all our brokenness and fragility, in the light of the mercy and acceptance of God. And it is the humility to accept that this is the path to our true selves; it is the liberation from our illusory and false self which urges bravado and ego, and the freedom to let God resurrect us from our broken selves into the person he is creating us to be.

The alternative to this contemplative attitude of self-accusation is self-justification. It is the constant assertion of our self on the world, and the constant illusion that we are good enough, useful enough, skilful enough and productive enough to justify our existence. We live in a culture that nurtures an attitude of self-justification. It is a culture built on a simple 'utilitarian logic... the logic of economics. Input leads to output. Effort leads to reward. Practice makes perfect. Pursue self-interest. Maximise utility. Impress the world.'[71] Following this 'utilitarian calculus' turns us into a 'shrewd animal, a crafty, self-preserving creature who is adept at playing the game'.[72]

Without contemplation we are constantly in peril from the lure of this 'utilitarian calculus' all around us. The church minister game is there to be played if we want to play it: a game of numbers and models and techniques, of performance and power and profile. There is a culture of self-justification in the modern Church where church leaders spend time and energy justifying their ministries under the guise of 'platform building'. A recent article refers to three church leaders:

An up-and-coming young leader buys 30,000 Twitter followers from a dubious website. Another seems to have a Wikipedia page set up for himself, full of the kind of obscure details you might expect on a full-blown celebrity profile. A third tells a friend, just starting out in ministry, that he should dedicate at least a third of his time to 'building your platform'.[73]

Is this not a case of church minister turned 'shrewd animal'; a case of people, each with a sincere vocation, resorting to techniques and temptations that promise accelerated success in their aims and ambitions? Is this not what happens when we fail to face up to the reality that our vocation requires more of us than we honestly think we are capable of? Instead of building a platform we should be building a booth like that of Jonah, sitting down in it, and asking God to help us see ourselves for who we truly are.

Contemplation is that deliberate willingness to face up to our own frailty, our own limitations. Contemplation is the willingness to enter the kind of space that engenders an honest assessment of our capabilities. It is the willingness to let go of all our pretences and take on the gift of humility. For in the economy of the kingdom we trust that only the path of humility will enable us to discover our true selves and the truest expression of our vocation within the plans of God.

Gardeners, midwives and artists

Three images have helped me to see the expression of a contemplative approach to life and ministry: those of a gardener, a midwife and an artist.

I have probably learnt as much about ministry and leadership from tending an allotment as anything else. As I described earlier, we took on an allotment some years ago, which turned out to offer little promise as a place to grow anything edible when we first dug into it. However, after the initial year of fighting with brambles, wasps and stones, and another year adding huge amounts of organic material to the soil, we finally began to see that it might be possible to enjoy the fruit (and veg) of all our work. By the spring of our third year we had about half a dozen raised beds containing material that was more soil than stone and which had already begun to show the potential of producing a crop.

I vividly remember a moment at the end of that spring when I had gone up to the allotment on a day off. It was a gorgeous day and I had headed off looking forward to a morning working hard to make progress on the allotment project. Earlier that spring we had managed to bring on all kinds of seedlings and had transplanted them carefully into the raised beds. After attending to various jobs that morning I stopped and sat at the edge of one of the raised beds. I began to think about the rest of the morning. And as I did a reality dawned on me. *There was nothing left to do!* Everything that I could possibly do to bring edible produce from this small area of former car park had been done. The only thing I could do now was to wait.

My response to this reality was two-fold. Firstly, frustration. The process of vegetable production no longer had need of me. I was superfluous. I was reduced to the role of spectator to a process I was increasingly feeling to be out of my control. But secondly, wonder. As I sat there looking at rows of seedlings imperceptibly growing in front of me, I began to wonder at the mysterious and extraordinary processes of nature that were at work in the soil and in the plants. That I was reduced to a non-active role and asked simply to wait, that there was nothing I could do but allow this slow, patient process to do its work, was not something to fight against but something to wonder at, rejoice in and go with. I had reached the end of my usefulness, but rather than feeling insignificant, I felt grateful. And in that moment, perhaps fancifully, I almost felt I could hear the life of the soil and the potential energy of the air and sun at work. Whatever that experience was, it was a sudden appreciation of my own finiteness in the context of a greater process. It was an experience of the grace of partnership, of participating humbly with forces and processes beyond me. It was an experience of the contemplative life.

The role of the midwife is not dissimilar to this. At the birth of both our children we were immensely impressed with the gentle but crucial work of the midwives. Theirs is a job of partnering with a process essentially beyond their control. Their skill lies in listening, to both mother and baby, and in timely and wise interventions. Their skill also lies in not asserting their will or agenda beyond the pace of the development of the baby they are tasked with delivering safely. Patience and humility in the context of a greater force and a larger concern are key.

When our first child was born we were a little more anxious about the outcome and in need of more assurance from the midwife. It was just after Christmas and I remember the two midwives in attendance sitting behind a curtain at one end of the room discussing the *EastEnders* omnibus edition of the day before! At the time I found this a little annoying. After all, wasn't the arrival of our first child a little more important than *EastEnders*? On the other hand, I now see it as a perfect image of the role of the midwife: gently present and deferential to the greater force of the birthing process, able to rest and relax as the process slowly took its course, yet close and ready to be fully present, and to intervene if the need arose.

Finally, the image of the artist. I have never been great with a paintbrush. However, I have consistently written poetry for some years. With time and experience I have begun to glimpse what many artists instinctively feel about their craft. Artists too feel this sense of collaboration with something beyond themselves. They also recognise the need to contain the self and restrain it from dominating the process. The best artists and the best art emerge out of humble participation with a creative process which is hard to locate, but which is very powerfully experienced. And the greatest art is the result not just of applied skill but of a deep attentiveness to the subject so as to get beyond mere representation and towards the essence, the inscape,[74] perhaps the soul of a subject. Former Dean of Westminster Michael Mayne wrote:

> How does an artist achieve this?... By paying attention. By the intentness of his looking. By achieving, through disciplining his eyes, that kind of cleansed perception that enables him to see into the life of things, and which is a real act of 'in-selfing'.[75]

Art, then, is the process of enabling us to see, the discipline of looking and paying attention to a subject, not to simply render a copy of it, but to imagine it in such a way that we see something true and revelatory about it. And in that attentiveness many artists testify to a deep sense of connection with something of the essence of the subject, beyond that which they are seeking to portray. Mayne observed:

> The creation of a work of art is not entirely one-sided. It demands that I, the observer, should be in some sense a *co-creator* by the gift of my time and my attention, for only then shall I feel something of the great mystery of the existence of what has been portrayed.[76]

When I began my current role as pioneer minister in the central area of Poole the task was described to me as an artistic one. 'We have a blank canvas and we're looking for an artist who can paint it,' was the gist of the remit. It was more than an idle metaphor. The work of an artist is one of deep attentiveness, patient observation and the investment of time and skill in a process of co-creation with the presence beyond the subject. To truly participate in the ministry of God, in this place at this time, requires precisely those skills and those attitudes.

Vocation and the contemplative life

How does a commitment to the contemplative life begin to shape our vocation? How does it begin to shape ministry and leadership? This is a huge question which perhaps warrants deeper exploration. A recent book by Ian Cowley, *The Contemplative Minister*, begins to explore this. Ian and I had a conversation which turned into a chapter in his book entitled 'Reconnect, a contemplative church'.[77] That Ian saw our small community as a worthy example of contemplative ministry was flattering, but also rather surprising. Reconnect certainly did not set out to be a contemplative church. We set out to be a missional community committed to incarnational ministry. That meant becoming deeply engaged with our community and deeply committed to listening, to a growing attentiveness to God at work in our community and in us. Our commitment to all of those things has given birth to something that perhaps you could call a contemplative church.

At Reconnect we are still learning, but a recent example might help give form to what we are exploring. As a community we reached something of a crossroads when we needed to find somewhere else to gather on a Sunday. We had grown used to using our café on Poole High Street, and having to find somewhere else left us feeling vulnerable. Throughout the life of Reconnect the leadership team had wrestled with the difficult dynamics of being a relatively small community and trying to embrace a pattern of community life that gave space for worship, discipleship and mission. It had felt as if we were never quite able to do all we would like to do. Providing for children within our life together had also proved stretching and had been a source of constant dilemma.

So as we met as a leadership team once again it felt that we were facing all the complexity of competing needs and hopes. We all felt as if we were trying to solve an equation which was beyond us. But growing, as we were, into a more contemplative approach to everything we do, I decided it was time to approach this dilemma differently. Our pattern in meetings such as these, not dissimilar perhaps to church meetings elsewhere, was to pray briefly, lay out the issues and discuss a way forward. Yet, this approach had never brought resolution, only an uncomfortable sense of awkward compromise. That evening I decided we were going to spend the first half of the meeting listening. First of all we gave each person an opportunity to simply state what they had done that day and how they were, so that each of us could listen to where people were at, and each person could be listened to. Then I read a short passage of scripture, a passage that seemed apt for where we were as a community. I invited us all to keep silent and listen to the voice of God. After about ten minutes I invited each person to say in a short sentence what they felt God was saying to them. We went round and did this without inviting comment. Then each person was invited to develop what they had said with reference to what they had heard from the others. Only then did we enter into discussion and attend to the issues we faced.

The result was revelatory and remarkable. We arrived at conclusions that surprised us and excited us. We found ourselves shaping our life together around a sense of God's vision and vocation for us as a community, rather than around the solution to a problem. The pattern of gathering that we arrived at that evening has produced a burst of life within the community of Reconnect. Those at the core of Reconnect have spoken about how life-giving their church community now feels. And we have been able to engage with a much greater number of people on the fringes of our community than ever before. I now conduct the majority of my leadership and other meetings like this, particularly those where complex and difficult decisions need to be made.[78]

However, before anyone looks to formulate this approach and transpose it into their own context, it needs to be clear that this mode of decision-making is the fruit of a commitment to the contemplative life. This book has arrived at an exploration of the dimensions of the contemplative life by travelling with Jonah on his journey to Nineveh. His journey has been one of a letting go of the illusions of control, identity and success and of the painful discovery of the possibilities of grace. As the story ends and Jonah sits in his rather pathetic booth at the periphery of the action, he is invited to reflect on all that has happened. He is given a choice: whether he wants to go deeper into this world of grace, or not. The world of grace, the contemplative life, requires much more of Jonah than even his highly responsible life in the court of Jeroboam II did. It will require downward mobility, a willingness continually to offer his ambitions to God in the forging of his vocation. It will require a willingness to embrace his own failings and his own darkness and trust that in that hard, often painful commitment, God will bring his transformation. It will require a deep commitment to people and place, an incarnational loving covenant with the context to which he is called, which shuns the temptation to treat it like a utility, but instead treats it like a sacred place where God is already at work. It will require a willingness to take his place on the edge of things, not constantly and heroically taking centre stage, in order to be attentive to God and to discipline the tendency to wrest control of ministry from God himself. And critically, it will require him to see his own transformation and personal formation, his own 'becoming', as part of his vocation. God's invitation to grace-filled contemplative living is an invitation to let God shape us in the context of our vocation, and to see our vocation as the context in which we are shaped.

It is the fullness of this invitation, lived out in individuals and communities, not primarily certain techniques of prayer or approaches to leading meetings, which will produce surprising new examples of life in those who accept that invitation. For it is, in essence, an invitation to let God take his place once again as the 'chief actor' in our vocation and ministry. It is an invitation to relinquish our grasp on the impressive-looking dials and flashing lights of the control panels of our enterprises and allow God's Holy Spirit room to work, in us and in the communities we serve. It is an invitation to the grace of our own becoming in the midst of ministry. It is welcoming the disarming truth that God does his best work through our willingness to humbly, vulnerably give of our frail and fragile selves.

There are no easy answers or pre-packaged solutions to the challenge of our vocation or to the sense of crisis experienced within the Western Church. We would do well to move away from seeking answers and towards asking the right questions. Jonah comes from a place of being the sort of person who gave right answers to the critical questions of the day and prospered by it. Yet the book of Jonah is really a story of questions, of ambiguity and uncertainty. It begins with the unspoken questions of what will happen to Jonah and to Nineveh, journeys through scenes of ambiguous tension and ends with a final question: 'Should I not have concern for the great city of Nineveh?' (Jonah 4:11).

And the genius of the author of Jonah is to leave that same unanswered question for us to address for ourselves. Should God not be concerned about your great city? Your community? Your ministry? Your vocation? Do you trust God with the call he has given you? Do you trust him enough to lay aside your strategies and listen to his? Do you trust him enough to show your vulnerabilities instead of playing the hero? Do you trust him enough to attend to the darkness we experience? Do you trust him enough to place yourself at the edge of the action? Do you trust him enough to do nothing, to rest, when there is nothing else you can do? Do you trust him enough to allow him to work beyond the limitations of your concept of him?

The author of Jonah takes a man of great certainty and throws him into chaos. The conclusion does not seem to be a new certainty, but rather a new question. A question about the nature of God, the character of God, and (most critically) the place he takes in our lives. Put simply, the 'answer' to all the questions of Jonah is not a new technique, a new plan, a new strategy; it is a renewed relationship. A renewed relationship with God that establishes the orbit of our aims, ambitions, hopes, dreams and our very selves around him. A renewed relationship that lays down all the props and illusions from within ourselves, and those projected onto us by others, in a consistent commitment to allow God himself to be the source of all our being and doing.

Notes

1   See for example Rabbi Joseph, 1965, available online at www.intro.teachtorah.org
2   Joseph Soloveitchik, *The Lonely Man of Faith* (Random House, 2006).
3   Soloveitchik, *The Lonely Man of Faith*, p. 45.
4   Soloveitchik, *The Lonely Man of Faith*, p. 27.
5   David Brooks, *The Road to Character* (Random House, 2015), p. x.
6   Pope Benedict XVI, *Deus Caritas Est, God is Love: First Encyclical Letter* (Catholic Truth Society, 2006), p. 5.
7   Pope Benedict XVI, *Deus Caritas Est*, p. 5.
8   Pope Benedict XVI, *Deus Caritas Est*, p. 14.
9   Brooks, *The Road to Character*, p. xi.
10 Quoted in Rowan Williams, *Silence and Honey Cakes* (Lion, 2003), p. 82.
11 Sheldon H. Blank, in Assembly of Rabbis of the Reformed Synagogues of Great Britain (eds.), *Forms of Prayer for Jewish Worship III, Prayers for the High Holydays Days of Awe*, 8th edition 5745 (London: Church House Publishing, 1985) p. 988, quoted in Rosemary Nixon, *The Message of Jonah* (IVP, 2003) p. 67.
12 Eiléan Ní Chuilleanáin, by kind permission of the author and The Gallery Press, Loughcrew, Oldcastle, County Meath, Ireland, from *Selected Poems*, 2008.
13 Eiléan Ní Chuilleanáin, from *Selected Poems*.
14 Quoted in Williams, *Silence and Honey Cakes*, p. 82.
15 Quoted in Eugene Peterson, *Under the Unpredictable Plant* (Eerdmans, 1992), pp. 20–21.
16 James Limburg, *Jonah* (Westminster/John Knox Press, 1993), p. 43.
17 Williams, *Silence and Honey Cakes*, p. 62.
18 Williams, *Silence and Honey Cakes*, p. 62.
19 Quoted in Nixon, *The Message of Jonah*, p. 73.
20 Richard Rohr, *Falling Upward* (SPCK, 2012), p. 66.
21 Rohr, *Falling Upward*, p. xviii.
22 Rohr, *Falling Upward*, p. 27.
23 Quoted in Rohr, *Falling Upward*, p. 136.
24 Nixon, *The Message of Jonah*, p. 100.
25 Michael Mayne, *Sunrise of Wonder* (DLT, 2008), p. 23.
26 John Ortberg, *The Life You've Always Wanted* (Zondervan, 1997), p. 76.
27 Quoted in Rohr, *Falling Upward*, p. 136.
28 Quoted in Rohr, *Falling Upward*, p. 65.
29 Brooks, *The Road to Character*, p. 252.
30 Brooks, *The Road to Character*, p. 11.
31 John V. Taylor, *The Easter God and His Easter People* (Continuum, 2003), p. 73.
32 Claus Westermann, *Praise and Lament in the Psalms* (John Knox Press, 1981).
33 Walter Brueggemann, *Spirituality of the Psalms* (Fortress Press, 2002).
34 Peterson, *Under the Unpredictable Plant*, p. 90.
35 Gerald May, *The Dark Night of the Soul* (Harper Collins, 2004), p. 73.
36 May, *The Dark Night of the Soul*, p. 68.
37 Barbara Brown Taylor, *Learning to Walk in the Dark* (Canterbury Press, 2014), p. 78.
38 For an exploration of this issue, see Paul Bradbury, *Sowing in Tears* (Grove, 2007).

39 Williams, *Silence and Honey Cakes*, p. 66.
40 Vincent J. Donovan, *Christianity Rediscovered* (SCM, 2001), p. xix.
41 Donovan, *Christianity Rediscovered*, p. 14.
42 Emil Brunner, quoted in John V. Taylor, *The Go-Between God* (SCM, 1972), p. 133.
43 Brené Brown, *Daring Greatly* (Penguin, 2012), p. 12.
44 Quoted in Williams, *Silence and Honey Cakes*, p. 89.
45 Quoted in Nixon, *The Message of Jonah*, p. 63.
46 Quoted in Robert Macfarlane, *The Wild Places* (Grant, 2007), p. 143.
47 David Runcorn, *Fear and Trust* (SPCK, 2011), p. 2.
48 C.S. Lewis, *Miracles* (Fount, 1977), p. 112.
49 Lewis, *Miracles*, p. 136.
50 Lewis, *Miracles*, p. 138.
51 Lewis, *Miracles*, p. 144.
52 Quoted in Williams, *Silence and Honey Cakes*, p. 89.
53 Williams, *Silence and Honey Cakes*, p. 89.
54 www.poolemc.org.uk/projects/space-for-life.
55 F. Rayns and T. Mansfield, *Living Soils—A Call to Action* (Soil Association, 2015). Available from www.soilassociation.org.
56 Peterson, *Under the Unpredictable Plant*, p. 135.
57 Williams, *Silence and Honey Cakes*, p. 98.
58 Thomas Keating, *Open Mind, Open Heart* (Continuum, 1986), p. 168, quoted in Ian Cowley, *The Contemplative Minister* (BRF, 2015), p. 97.
59 The cry of the unicorn on entering the new Narnia in C.S. Lewis' *The Last Battle* (Collins, 1998), p. 207.
60 Eugene Peterson, *The Contemplative Pastor* (Eerdmans, 1989), p. 104.
61 Taylor, *The Go-Between God*, p. 3.
62 David Runcorn, *The Road to Growth Less Travelled* (Grove, 2008), p. 21.
63 Thomas Merton, *New Seeds of Contemplation* (Continuum, 1999), p. 15.
64 Merton, *New Seeds of Contemplation*, p. 13.
65 Derek Mahon, *Selected Poems* (Penguin, 1990), p. 62.
66 A phrase I first came across in May, *The Dark Night of the Soul*, p. 130.
67 Taylor, *The Go-Between God*, p. 69.
68 Richard Rohr, *Immortal Diamond* (SPCK, 2013), p. 71.
69 Stephen Cottrell, *Hit the Ground Kneeling* (CHP, 2008), p. 1.
70 Cottrell, *Hit the Ground Kneeling*, p. 2.
71 Brooks, *The Road to Character*, p. x.
72 Brooks, *The Road to Character*, p. xi.
73 Martin Saunders, 'Platform: Why a Culture of Self-Promotion Threatens to Throttle the Church', 2015, via www.christiantoday.com.
74 A word invented by the Jesuit priest and poet Gerald Manley Hopkins to describe the complex characteristics that give each thing its uniqueness and that differentiate it from other things.
75 Mayne, *Sunrise of Wonder*, pp. 153–54.
76 Mayne, *Sunrise of Wonder*, p. 159, emphasis mine.
77 Cowley, *The Contemplative Minister*, pp. 136–44.
78 This approach to meetings was inspired by Mark Yaconelli's *Contemplative Youth Ministry* (SPCK, 2006), see particularly chapter 10.t

Also from BRF…

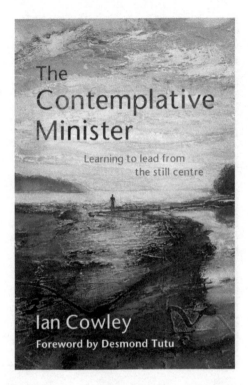

At one time Christian ministry offered the opportunity to spend your life in the study of God's word, in reading and reflection, in prayer and sermon preparation, and in the faithful pastoral care of a community. These days there are very few jobs in full-time ministry which do not require a heroic combination of stamina, multi-tasking and change management. Drawing on his experience of developing and leading relevant training programmes, Ian Cowley assesses the stresses and pressures of the job and shows how to grow into a 'contemplative minister', prioritising a relationship of deepening love with God.

The Contemplative Minister
Learning to lead from the still centre
Ian Cowley
978 0 85746 360 9 £8.99

brfonline.org.uk

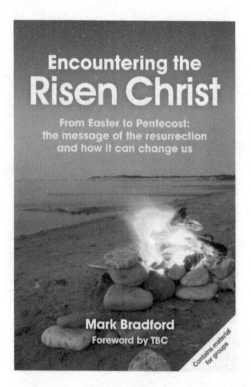

How can we encounter the risen Lord Jesus in a life-transforming way? How can we be equipped and strengthened to share the message of the resurrection with the world? The post-resurrection encounters between Jesus and the disciples provide us with some of the most profound and personal moments to be found in scripture. The risen Christ comes to his disciples in all their brokenness—their sadness, fear, doubt, shattered dreams and failure—and calls them to a future filled with hope, confidence, confirmed faith, new beginnings and restored lives.

Encountering the Risen Christ
From Easter to Pentecost: the message of the resurrection and how it can change us
Mark Bradford
978 0 85746 428 6 £7.99

brfonline.org.uk

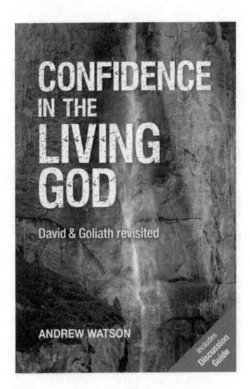

Confidence lies at the heart of society, determining the success or failure of the economy, the government, companies, schools, churches and individuals. As Christians, we are called to proclaim our faith in God, but how can we build and maintain this confidence in an increasingly secularised culture where such faith is often seen as marginal, embarrassing or even downright dangerous? Using the story of David and Goliath as his starting point, Andrew Watson shows how the Lord can indeed be our confidence, whatever the odds.

Confidence in the Living God
David and Goliath revisited
Andrew Watson
978 0 85746 482 8 £7.99

brfonline.org.uk

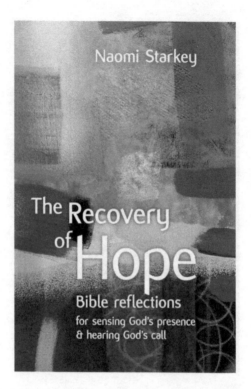

We live in the hope of experiencing first-hand the all-sufficient grace, love and forgiveness which are God's alone, a hope that we may know with our heads long before we feel it in our hearts. Such hope may mean encountering God as consoling presence in the darkness, as well as one who challenges us to respond to his call. That call may prove to be costly but, in responding, we are transformed by discovering and rediscovering that we are known exactly as we are, yet still loved beyond understanding, as God's precious children. In a series of Bible reflections—and some poems—this hope is explored in different ways, from the yearning of the psalmist to walking the gentle journey of the Good Shepherd's leading.

The Recovery of Hope
Bible reflections for sensing God's presence and hearing God's call
Naomi Starkey
978 0 85746 417 0 £8.99

brfonline.org.uk